English *for* REAL ESTATE

SHORT COURSE SERIES

Peter Altmann and Alice Jovy

Cornelsen

Impressum

Verfasser: Peter Altmann, Wien; Alice Jovy, München
Berater: Joseph Genlloud, München
Projektleitung: Rebecca Syme
Außenredaktion und Koordination: James Copeland
Redaktionelle Mitarbeit: Mindy Ehrhart Krull
Layoutkonzept: finedesign, Berlin
Technische Umsetzung: zweiband.media, Berlin
Umschlagsgestaltung: Jan Haux / Pepe Jürgens, Berlin

www.cornelsen.de

1. Auflage, 1. Druck 2015

Basierend auf English for Real Estate ISBN 978-3-464-20006-3

Alle Drucke dieser Auflage sind inhaltlich unverändert und können im Unterricht nebeneinander verwendet werden.

Druck: AZ Druck und Datentechnik GmbH, Kempten

ISBN: 978-3-464-20340-8

PEFC
PEFC/04-31-2260

PEFC zertifiziert
Dieses Produkt stammt aus nachhaltig bewirtschafteten Wäldern und kontrollierten Quellen.
www.pefc.de

Table of Contents

		Topics	Useful Language
	1 **Choosing a Location** Page 6	• real estate vs. commercial properties • carrying out a location analysis • planning boards and the approval process	• saying where things are • prepositions of place • asking about and describing a location • American vs. British English
	2 **Professions in Real Estate** Page 14	• job profiles and descriptions of real estate professions • investment profiles • appraisers and the appraisal process	• telephoning • making sentences more polite • spelling out email addresses
	3 **Viewing the Property** Page 24	• describing a property • giving sales particulars • market reports	• describing property • locating rooms • saying numbers and measurements
	4 **Financing Property** Page 32	• valuation methods • analyzing financial strength • lending, borrowing, and loan applications • acquiring property in the UK	• interviewing a client • saying numbers and formulas • vocabulary of loans and mortgages
	5 **Buying, Selling, and Leasing** Page 40	• due diligence • letters of intent • tenancy agreements • purchase agreements	• terminology of leasing • conditionals • language of negotiation
	6 **Managing Property** Page 50	• asset, property, and facility management • service charges • tenant relations • trade professions	• presenting your company • taking messages • vocabulary of service charge statements

Page 58–61 Partner Files
Page 62–67 Transcripts
Page 68–71 Answer Key
Page 72–73 Phrases to Use
Page 74 Key Verbs in Context
Page 75 American English vs. British English
Page 76–79 A–Z Wordlist
Page 80 Tracklist

Introducing *English for Real Estate*

English is an essential part of working in real estate today. This is especially true as property development and investment become more international, with English as the common language of global business. For agents, investors, asset and property managers, lawyers, and others in the real estate sector, this book will help build stronger relationships with colleagues and business partners.

English for Real Estate has been specifically designed to help you build confidence when using English as part of your professional life. The book's six units cover the topics, skills, and vocabulary that will help you develop your competence in situations such as speaking with agents, negotiating with tenants, describing investment opportunities, and handling property management.

- The units build on realistic scenarios that draw from a range of situations and highlight different ways of communicating, such as meetings, phone calls, emails, and informal conversations. A variety of exercises accompany these excerpts to allow you to put the skills and phrases you have learned into practice.
- Listening exercises in each unit, found on the accompanying CD, are a key feature of the book and provide you with vital listening practice. The exercises present a range of accents to improve your listening skills and reflect the way English is used as a lingua franca in business.
- The book encourages you to practice your real estate skills with other people in your English course or with your instructor. The Partner Files give you the opportunity to immerse yourself in realistic situations while practicing key skills and language.
- At the back of the book, you will find a comprehensive list of Phrases to Use to refer to when doing the communicative exercises as well as in professional situations. Transcripts for the listening activities, an Answer Key, an A–Z Wordlist, and a Vocabulary Bank are provided to assist you as you work through the book.

The Needs Analysis on the next page will support you when working through the book. It will help you set personal learning goals and assess your progress as you work through the material in the book.

We hope you enjoy working through the book and that it helps you develop your skills and build your confidence.

Peter Altmann
Alice Jovy

Needs Analysis

English for Real Estate is designed to improve your ability to use English in your professional life. However, you are in the best position to know what language and skills you need to develop to help you in your work.

Look at the lists below and spend a few minutes selecting the items that you consider most important. Which do you want to prioritize and improve? Add other items to the lists that you would like to concentrate on.

need more practice

have made good progress

Real estate language and skills

Describing property and professions in real estate

- Discussing plans with a visitor
- Offering refreshments
- Explaining a building's layout

Buying, selling, leasing, and financing property

- Describing the terms of a loan
- Explaining sales procedures
- Writing a letter of intent
- Negotiating a purchase agreement

Managing property

- Describing management roles
- Explaining service charges
- Practice with tenant relations

Try to keep the language and skills you want to improve in mind while working with the book. Once you have completed the book, turn back to this page and assess your progress.

In this unit you will …
- review property types and describe locations
- practice saying where things are
- learn words and phrases related to planning
- read about British vs. American real estate terms

1 Choosing a Location

Do you agree or disagree with the following statements? Compare your answers with your partner's.

		Agree	Disagree
1	Real estate is something that can be traded like silver, gold, or any other asset.	☐	☐
2	Investing in real estate is one of the best ways to reduce tax payments.	☐	☐
3	Real estate is a more reliable investment than a savings account.	☐	☐
4	The three most important factors when choosing real estate are *location, location, location*.	☐	☐
5	Potential rental income is more important than the quality of a property's structure or architectural design.	☐	☐
6	Real estate investment offers excellent opportunities for diversification, unlike other assets.	☐	☐

1 Decide which types of property are *residential* and which are *commercial*. Write them in the correct column.

apartment/flat (BE) • condominium (AE) / commonhold (BE) • hotel • house • office space • logistics center • shopping mall (AE) / shopping centre (BE) • townhouse (AE) / terraced house (BE)

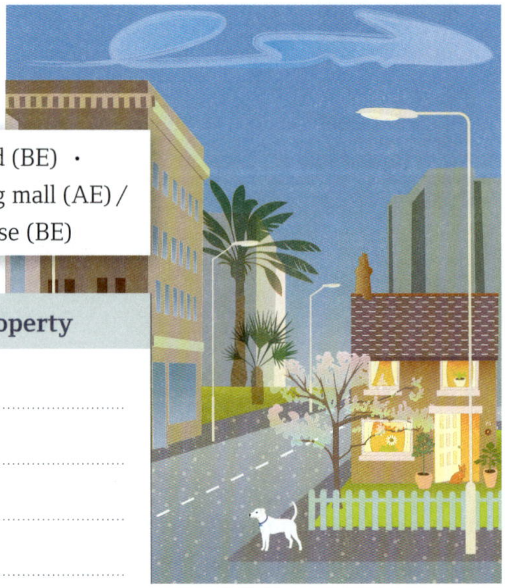

Residential property	Commercial property
....	....
....	....
....	....
....	....

Can you think of any other types of property that you could add to the table?

2 Look at the list of location factors and rank their importance (5 is the most important) when choosing your own home. Compare your answers with your partner's.

	1	2	3	4	5
Distance to supermarkets and stores					
Distance to workplace					
Garage or parking lot					
Friendly and helpful neighbors					
Distance to open space and parks					
Amount of traffic					
Availability of public transportation					
Distance to the city center					
Low crime rate					
Quality of schools					

Which additional location factors are important to you?

3 **Match 1–8 with a–h to form word pairs. Then match the word pairs to their definitions (A–H).**

1 bike	a lot
2 commercial	b location
3 location	c lanes
4 parking	d zone
5 pedestrian	e district
6 prime	f analysis
7 public	g location
8 secondary	h transportation

Remember that certain terms in American English are different in British English. For example, "parking lot" (AE) and "car park" (BE), or "subway" (AE) and "underground" (BE).

A *bike lanes* .... special paths for bicycles

B .... a report which provides a detailed description of an area

C .... the bus, subway, or train

D .... a prestigious or desirable area

E .... an area that does not obtain the highest value

F .... a place where people can leave their cars

G .... an area without car traffic

H .... an area of a town or city with stores and businesses

4 🔊02 **Richard Hewes works for an international real estate company. Listen to the advice he gives a client on finding commercial property, and then tick the sentences that he says, either in Column A or Column B.**

	A	B
1	☐ I think that the importance of finding a good location cannot be underestimated.	☐ I think that the importance of finding a good location cannot be overestimated.
2	☐ In other words, a large number of potential customers should be able to see your business.	☐ In other words, you should be able to see a large number of potential customers.
3	☐ The best streets, of course, are those with a lot of traffic.	☐ The best streets, of course, are those with a lot of foot traffic.
4	☐ Are there other businesses nearby that will compete with you for customers?	☐ Are there other businesses near you that will compete for your business?
5	☐ This is why doing a location analysis is so important before making a decision.	☐ This is why doing a location analysis is so important after making a decision.

Words you need

to compete in Wettbewerb stehen
competition Konkurrenz
foot traffic (AE) / footfall (BE) Passantenfrequenz, Fußgängerverkehr
neighborhood nahe Umgebung
over-/underestimated über-/unterschätzt
visible sichtbar

5 🔊02 **Listen again to Richard's advice, and then complete the email.**

From: Richard Hewes
To: Olivia Woodson
Subject: **Location Analysis Services**

Dear Ms. Woodson,

Thank you for your interest in our services.

It was a pleasure to speak with you by phone yesterday, and to tell you a little bit about the importance of doing a location analysis.

As I explained, you need to keep several factors in mind when looking for a location for your business. To summarize, here are the four points I feel are most important:

1 ....

2 ....

3 ....

4 ....

I look forward to discussing your needs in more detail. Please let me know when you're available, and we can arrange a meeting at our offices.

Best regards,
Richard Hewes

Phrases to use

Saying where things are

North, south, east, west

- Winchester is / lies (to the) west of London.
- The site is a few miles east of the village.
- New York's Battery Park is on the southernmost tip of Manhattan.

***By* means *next to*.**

- There is a building by the lake.

To identify where places are located in a multistory building, use *on*.

- The gym is on the second floor.

For roads and rivers, use *on*.

- The town is located on the A25.
- The office complex is located directly on the Thames.

Nearby* means *in der Nähe*, and *near sth.* means *in der Nähe von etw.

- If you're hungry, there's a nice restaurant nearby.
- There's a bus stop on that street, and a subway station is also nearby.
- The hotel is near the business park.
- The business park is near the airport.

***To face* means *to be positioned toward*.**

- The balcony faces west.
- This window faces north.

***Opposite* and *across* mean *on the other side*.**

- Our office is opposite the supermarket.
- The parking lot is across the street.

6 Choose the correct word or phrase in each sentence.

1 There is a parking lot **to | of | by** the building site.
2 Let's meet **in | at | to** the corner of Kurfürstendamm and Uhlandstraße.
3 Wiesbaden lies **in | to | at** the west of Frankfurt.
4 Our office is **to | in | on** the fifth floor.
5 The property is a few miles south **of | from | by** the village.
6 The building site is situated **opposite of | opposite by | opposite** a school.
7 The hotel is **near of | nearby | near** the Vienna Opera House.

7 Working with a partner, describe where your home or office is located. If possible, use a map of your town or city. Try to use phrases from the box above.

8 **A real estate professional is giving a presentation to potential clients about the planning board approval process. Read the excerpt from the presentation and fill in the gaps with the words in the box.**

conditions · construction · permits · process · protected · reviewed · standard · structures

Now let's talk about the planning board and the approval ....[1] necessary for all new real estate projects. You might be surprised to hear this, but the planning board can be your friend! If you have questions about land-use plans, conservation areas, listed buildings, or any ....[2] trees on the property, it will be able to help you research and answer those questions.

Of course, the planning board is also there to monitor all ....[3] projects in the community. So you will have to get permission from the board for any new buildings or alterations to existing ....[4]. To get permission, you have to submit an application, which can be a complex and detailed process. The application allows the planning board to determine if the building is in line with the community's land-use plan, and if the work is going to follow ....[5] rules of construction. Despite international differences, the procedures for obtaining planning permission are similar in most countries, and every application goes through a well-defined process.

After the planning board has ....[6] the application, it will either be approved, approved subject to ....[7], or rejected. If rejected, the application may be appealed. And if you think you can perform construction work without an approved application, think again: any work carried out without the necessary ....[8] could be subject to demolition – at the owner's expense!

Words you need

land-use plan Bebauungsplan
listed building denkmalgeschütztes Gebäude
to monitor beobachten
planning board Bauamt

Now decide if the statements are true or false.

	True	False
1 The planning board is not allowed to answer questions about conservation areas.	☐	☐
2 Each country has a completely different process for applying for construction permits.	☐	☐
3 Applications to the planning board have to show that construction will be done correctly.	☐	☐
4 If the application is rejected, there is no possibility for appeal, and the construction will never happen.	☐	☐
5 If you build without the approval of the planning board, the structure may be demolished.	☐	☐

9 **Fill in the letters to form words from the presentation excerpt.**

1 l _ s _ _ d   _ u _ l _ _ _ g (a protected structure)
2 _ l _ _ r _ t i _ _ _ (changes to an existing building)
3 s _ _ _ _ _ t   _ o   _ o n _ _ _ _ o _ s (provisional approval)
4 _ e _ o _ i _ i o _ (controlled destruction of a building)

Now use the words to complete the sentences.

a The ………………………… of the old factory was more costly than expected, which caused the new construction to be delayed.

b Before moving into their new offices, the company wanted to make some ………………………… to the interior.

c Because the store was located in a …………………………………………, they needed special permission before installing new windows.

d Our application to the planning commission has been approved …………………………………………, which means that we have to make some changes to our construction plan before proceeding.

Language Traps

Sometimes a word in English may remind you of a similar word in German. In some cases, however, these words may have different meanings. Compare the German expressions on the left with the English expressions on the right.

Immobilienobjekt, Objekt Ich habe heute zwei *Objekte* besichtigt.	**property** I viewed two *properties* today.
Rückseite Der Eingang befindet sich an der *Rückseite* des Gebäudes.	**back, rear** The entrance is at the *rear* of the building.
gute Adresse Zehlendorf ist eine *gute Adresse* in Berlin.	**good location** Zehlendorf is a *good location* in Berlin.

Note the spelling: *A**d**resse* in German but *a**dd**ress* in English.

10 03 **Listen to Olivia showing a friend the space she has rented, and then match the words (1–6) with their definitions (a–f).**

1 broker
2 competition
3 foot traffic
4 layout
5 purchasing power
6 traffic

a the floor plan or arrangement of the interior
b the ability to buy goods and services
c the movement of vehicles through an area
d people or companies that offer similar products or services to the same customers
e the number of pedestrians passing by during a given period of time
f another word for agent

Listen again. Which of the factors in the box were mentioned? Circle them.

quality of schools · competition · sufficient parking · distance to central business district · lifestyle of local residents · distance to parks · accessibility · foot traffic · low crime rate

Words you need

frequency Häufigkeit
no kidding! im Ernst!
pleasant angenehm
tremendous enorm

Which factors are used for both commercial and residential property?

11 **Work with a partner to practice dialogues between an agent and a client.**

▷ Partner File 1: Partner A, page 58 / Partner B, page 60

Note the difference between "customer" and "client": generally, a customer is someone who buys goods from a store or restaurant, and a client is someone who receives professional services.

Phrases to use

Asking questions about a location

- What's the floor space? / How large is it? / How many square meters is it?
- Is it close to public transportation?
- How far is it from the city center?
- What kind of parking facilities are there?
- What other businesses/ companies/stores are nearby?

Describing a location

- The building is 1,000 square meters / has 1,000 square meters of usable space.
- It's located directly on the harbor.
- There are several subway/bus lines nearby.
- It's near / close to / adjacent to / next to the train station.
- There is a parking lot/ garage across the street.

The Language of Business

How do you say *Fachmarktzentrum* in English? Well, it depends which English you're using ...

A common type of commercial property in Germany is the *Fachmarktzentrum*. You're probably familiar with this kind of property. It's a group of stores placed together near a large parking lot, and the stores are normally placed side-by-side in a large, single-story structure. They are often located outside the city limits, and you need a car to get there.

But what do you call a *Fachmarktzentrum* in English? Well, it depends. As with a lot of real estate vocabulary, there are different terms used in the United States and the United Kingdom. For this reason, we refer to American English (AE) and British English (BE). For example, the AE word for *Fachmarktzentrum* is *strip mall* or *shopping center*, and in BE it's called a *retail park*.

Now let's look at another word, *Einkaufszentrum*, which also describes a building with many different stores. An *Einkaufszentrum* is normally enclosed so that the stores are all together in one large interior space. The English translations for this word are *shopping mall* (AE) and *shopping centre* (BE).

Wait a second! So, what exactly does the phrase *shopping center* mean in English? It depends if you're in an American or a British context. *Shopping centre* (in Britain) means *Einkaufszentrum*, and *shopping center* (in America) means *Fachmarktzentrum*.

But don't worry. Normally the differences between AE and BE are not so confusing. And most of the time, the words are exactly the same. For example, the term *department store (Kaufhaus)* is used on both sides of the Atlantic – whether it's Bloomingdale's in New York or Harrods in London.

Words you need

city limits Stadtgrenzen
enclosed inliegend, überdacht
single-story einstöckig
structure Gebäude

Complete the table to practice the terms discussed in the article.

German	AE	BE
Fachmarktzentrum		
Einkaufszentrum		
Kaufhaus		

Over to you

- A common way to make sure someone understands the phrase you're using is to give an example ("It's a department store, like KaDeWe"). What other techniques can you think of to avoid confusion when using real estate terms?
- When you speak to native English speakers, can you identify their country of origin? If you're not sure, what is a polite way of asking?

In this unit you will …
- review different real estate professions
- practice making sentences more polite
- practice reading email addresses
- read about the work of an appraiser

2 Professions in Real Estate

Use the words in the box to complete the sentences. Do you agree with the statements? Compare your answers with your partner's.

agent · appraiser · banker · lawyer · owner

1. The appraiser is the only professional in the real estate business who is 100 % objective.
2. As a banker, I don't have a good understanding of the technical aspects of real estate. I'm just focused on the financial side.
3. As a property owner, I don't have the time to speak with tenants or manage day-to-day matters.
4. You usually need a lawyer to amend a lease, but they're always too expensive. The changes they make to contracts don't justify their high fees.
5. I am not sure whether my agent is doing enough to earn his fee. All he does is introduce me to properties without providing any other services.

1 **Read the job profiles (A–H) and match the words in italics to the expressions (1–8, page 15).**

A My job is to look after property on behalf of my clients. I *liaise* with tenants, organize contractors and maintenance, and collect the rent from tenants.

B We invest in new developments or *refurbish* existing properties.

C Our clients are investors and developers who do not have enough equity to buy property without borrowing money. My role involves checking the clients' *credit standing*. Before we offer a loan, we establish whether it will be a good investment for the client and the bank.

D I identify investment opportunities, calculate the returns, undertake due diligence, and *negotiate* the best possible deal with the vendor.

E My clients are property owners. They hire me to formulate a business strategy and to identify any *opportunities* to enhance the value of their property.

F My main tasks include advising clients on the legal aspects of buying, selling, and leasing property, and making sure that the documents are in order. I also check the registry of deeds and the *title deeds*, as well as the implications these might have for my clients.

G We advise investors and *vendors* on the acquisition, development, and disposal of commercial property, and introduce these parties to one another.

H I examine development and alteration applications to assess whether they *comply with* zoning and land use regulations.

1 credit standing .... a bank's evaluation of a client's finances
2 title deeds .... documents which prove the legal right to own property
3 comply with .... follow (*here:* follow the law)
4 opportunities .... improve
5 refurbish .... possibilities
6 negotiate vendors .... sellers
7 liaise .... communicate
8 negotiate .... discuss (in order to reach an agreement)

Now match the job profiles (A–H) to the appropriate job titles.

D ...... acquisitions manager
C ...... loan officer (in a bank)
E ...... asset manager
A ...... property manager
B ...... developer
G ...... (real estate) agent/broker
F ...... property lawyer
H ...... city/town planner

For more about the words "lease", "let", and "rent", see page 41.

Words you need

alteration Umbau, Umgestaltung
contractor Bauunternehmer/in
developer Bauträger/in, Projektentwickler/in
disposal Veräußerung, Verkauf
equity Eigenkapital
land use Flächennutzung
to lease (AE) mieten, pachten
maintenance Instandhaltung, Wartung
to negotiate verhandeln
property manager Immobilienverwalter/in
registry of deeds Grundbuchamt
return Rendite
zoning Flächenwidmung

2 04 **Julia Lindsay is a property manager who is on a conference call with her client, Kurt Neumann, and a lawyer, Leah Taube. Listen to their conversation and complete the dialogue.**

Julia Hello. Sorry I'm a few minutes late calling in. I was ....[1].

Kurt No problem. How's everything going?

Julia Oh, fine, thanks. It's just been a busy day!

Kurt Well, glad you could join us. Leah Taube is also on the line. She worked on an SPA for us last month, and is going to be handling our real estate investments from now on.

Julia Hi, Leah, nice to meet you.

Leah Likewise.

Kurt In fact, Leah and I were just discussing the ....[2] for the Lehmann property.

Julia Ah, of course. Let me pull that up on my computer as well. OK, here it is. I'm looking at the version that was emailed on Tuesday; is that the same one you have?

Kurt Yes, that's right. And basically everything looks good to me. I just had a few questions about some of the details.

Julia OK, ...[3]?

Kurt Well, I think we should clarify certain aspects regarding tenant and landlord obligations for the property.

Leah Yes, I agree. For instance, there's a section on repairs. It should be much more detailed. It should specify who's responsible for repairs to ....[4] fixtures.

Kurt I think there should also be more information about the service charges, and which costs are recoverable from the tenant.

Julia Those are all good points. Also, I was speaking to one of the prospective tenants this week, and he wanted to bring in an architect to make ....[5]. I'm not sure that's covered in the lease.

Leah Actually, we have a section on alterations, if you look at the last paragraph on page three.

Julia Ah, yes, I see that now. But should that be expanded to include structural alterations?

Kurt Sorry, Julia, to include what?

Julia Structural alterations, such as changes to the roof, façade, or ....[6].

Kurt Yes, that's a good idea.

Leah OK, well, I suggest I work on a new draft of the lease, if that's all right with you two. I can have it ready for you by next Friday.

Kurt That would be great – thanks, Leah!

Listen again and check your answers.

Words you need

fixtures Ausstattung
likewise ebenfalls
load-bearing lasttragend
prospective potenziell
recoverable erstattungsfähig
service charges Nebenkosten
SPA (sales and purchase agreement) Kaufvertrag

Did you know?

Agents and brokers

Real estate brokers are also called real estate agents. In the US, a *realtor®* is a protected name for real estate agents who are members of the National Association of Realtors®. In the UK, they are generally called *estate agents* if they work with residential property, or *agents/brokers* if they work with commercial property.

Phrases to use

Offering help

- What can I do for you?
- How can I help you?

Suggestions

- How about ...?
- Would ... suit you?
- Is ... convenient for you?

Softening bad news

- Sorry, but ...
- I'm afraid ... (I can't make it on Friday.)
- Unfortunately, ...
- Actually, ...

How to make sentences more polite

In English, suggestions and requests tend to be less direct than in some other languages. In order to avoid sounding impolite, study these polite phrases.

Confirming

- Yes, of course.
- Sure, no problem.
- Certainly!
- Two o'clock is fine.
- I look forward to seeing you then.

Requests

- Could I possibly ...?
- Could I ask you to ...?
- Is there any chance ...?
- I was hoping ...
- I was wondering if ...?
- Would you mind ...?

Remember that "I was wondering" means "Ich habe mich gefragt" – not "~~Ich habe mich gewundert~~".

3 **Read the extract from a telephone conversation between Leonard Woodward, a real estate broker, and Tina Hopp, a property lawyer. Change Leonard's statements to make them more polite.**

Leonard ~~Woodward. Who is it?~~ *Leonard Woodward speaking. How can I help you?* 1

Tina Hello, Mr. Woodward. This is Tina Hopp from Newland & Houston. I was wondering if we could go over the SPA for the warehouse sometime soon. Is Friday convenient?

Leonard No, it's impossible! Only Monday. 2

Tina Yes, that's fine. How about the morning?

Leonard 11:30! 3

Tina Oh, I'm afraid that's a bit too late for me. Is there any chance we could meet earlier?

Leonard When? 4

Tina Is 8:00 convenient for you?

Leonard Yes. 5

Tina Where shall we meet?

Leonard My office. 6

Tina Could I have your address?

Leonard I thought you had it. It's Tellweg 120. 7

Tina Could you spell Tellweg for me, please?

Leonard I said T-e-l-l-w-e-g! 8

Tina OK, thanks. So see you on Monday at 8:00 a.m. then.

Leonard Yes! 9

Lawyers vs. notaries

A lawyer involved in property matters in the UK is also called a *solicitor*. In the US a lawyer may also be called an *attorney*. Lawyers look after the conveyancing *(Eigentumsübertragung)* of property – i.e., the legal process of transferring ownership from one person to another.

In German-speaking countries, only a *Notar* (in English, *notary*) can carry out property transactions. However, in the UK and the US, the job of a notary is to authenticate signatures and certify copies of documents. They can be lawyers, but they might not specialize in real estate.

4 **An acquisitions manager (A) receives a call from a real estate agent (B). Work with a partner to make an arrangement using the instructions.**

A Answer the phone.

B Ask to speak to the acquisitions manager responsible for real estate investments on the East Coast.

A Say you are the acquisitions manager

B Say you are a real estate agent and have an office tower in Gilford. You are calling because you believe this may fit the company's investment profile.

A Say you would be interested in seeing the sales details. Ask if an appraisal is available.

B Explain that a signed confidentiality agreement is required to see the sales details.

A Agree to the confidentiality agreement. Provide email address where it can be sent.

B Read back email address.

A Confirm that it is correct.

B Say thank you and when you will send the sales details.

Did you know?

People often answer the phone by saying their full or first name, but not by using only their family name. In a business environment, you often hear something like "Hello, Five Star Real Estate, Mary (Phillips) speaking. How can I help you?"

At home, people just say "Hello".

Language Traps

German	English
Termin Ich habe nächste Woche einen *Termin* mit einem potenziellen Kunden.	**appointment, meeting** I've got an *appointment* with a prospective client next week.
Rendezvous Ich habe heute Abend ein *Rendezvous* mit meiner neuen Freundin.	**date** I've got a *date* with my new girlfriend tonight.
aktuell Ist das die *aktuelle* Version?	**current** Is this the *current* version?
eigentlich, tatsächlich Was ist das *eigentliche* Problem?	**actual** What is the *actual* problem?
griffbereit, praktisch Haben Sie die Adresse *griffbereit*?	**handy** Do you have the address *handy*?
Handy, Mobiltelefon Ich gebe Ihnen meine *Handy*nummer.	**cell phone (AE), mobile (BE)** Let me give you my *cell phone* number.
Büro Er ist gerade nicht im *Büro*.	**office (not: bureau = Behörde)** He's not in the *office* at the moment.
Exposé Ich schicke Ihnen das *Exposé* gleich morgen früh.	**sales details, rental details** I'll send you the *sales details* first thing tomorrow morning.

5 **Correct the mistakes in the sentences.**

1 My bureau is on the second floor.
2 Sorry! I can't see you tomorrow. I have a date with my boss.
3 Could I have your handy number, please?
4 I'm afraid this version of the location analysis isn't actual.

Translate the sentences into English.

1 Ihr Handy klingelt! ....

2 Rufen Sie bitte in meinem Büro an. ....

3 Teilen Sie mir bitte den aktuellen Stand des Projekts mit.

....

4 Ich möchte Ihnen gerne das Exposé zu diesem Objekt schicken.

....

6 05 **Leah Taube calls Julia Lindsay. Listen to their conversation, and then fill in Julia's email address and the subject line.**

From: leah_taube@fastmail.ch

To: ....

Subject: ....

Now use words from the box to complete Leah's email message to Julia.

clarify · feedback · finalize · mentioned · particular · regards · repairs · specifically

Dear Ms. Lindsay,

As I ....[1] to you on the phone earlier today, there's a new version of the lease for the Lehmann property. I'm attaching it as a PDF document. Please take a look and let me know if you have any comments or questions.

Kurt has ....[2] asked me to ....[3] the section on service charges. You will see there's a new paragraph which does this on page 5. There is also a new section on ....[4] on page 7. Please take a look at this new language in ....[5].

We would like to ....[6] the lease no later than the first of the month, so please respond as soon as you can with your ....[7].

Best ....[8],

Leah Taube

7 06 **Spell out the email addresses (1–4). Listen and check your answers.**

1 leah_taube@fastmail.ch
2 m.pisecky@immob_advice.at
3 andrew.leicester@jvw-consulting.com
4 ekkehardt.richter@wohn_linie.de

Now listen to four email addresses and write them down.

5 ....

6 ....

7 ....

8 ....

Did you know?

In English we use the following expressions when reading out email addresses.

German	**English**
Unterstrich	underscore
Minus (in E-Mails)	dash/hyphen
Punkt (in E-Mails)	dot
Kleinschrift	lowercase
Großschrift	uppercase

Give your own email address and phone number to a partner. Check that he/she has written them down correctly, then switch roles.

8 Put the words into the correct order to make questions that a real estate agent might ask when creating an investment profile for a new client.

1 are | currently | for | looking | property | type | what | you | of

2 are | focusing | geographical | on | regions | what | you

3 did | have | in | investment | mind | volume | of | what | you

4 require | level | occupancy | of | do | what | you

5 location | what | are | factors | most | the | important

Now fill in the gaps in the investment profile with the headings in the box.

Property Type · Investment Volume · Occupancy Rate · Location Factors · Country

Immobilienfonds
Investment Profile

Otto Brenner · Goldgasse 59 · 61030 Frankfurt · Tel: + 49 69 62 8803

International Acquisitions

A ....
Austria, Czech Republic, Germany, Switzerland, the Netherlands

B ....
Central Business Districts (CBDs), peripheral business districts with excellent amenities

C ....
Commercial buildings (office and logistics)

D ....
Minimum investment € 10–15 million

E ....
Not less than 80 %

Which questions above (1–5) match each of the headings (A–E)?

9 Work with a partner to discuss possible investments.

▷ Partner File 2: Partner A, page 58 / Partner B, page 60

10 07 Listen to a real estate specialist discuss different professions, and then match the professions with the tasks.

agent/broker ▢ ▢ ▢

lawyer ▢ ▢ ▢

architect ▢

building contractor ▢ ▢

appraiser ▢ ▢

property manager ▢ ▢ ▢

1 ensures rent is paid on time
2 does the building construction work
3 undertakes due diligence
4 draws plans for a new building
5 draws up contracts
6 oversees lease renewals
7 identifies potential investment opportunities
8 shows clients around properties
9 assists clients in finding property that meets their requirements
10 undertakes a title search
11 prepares sales particulars
12 calculates the viability of an investment
13 oversees leasing of vacant properties
14 inspects the condition of a building
15 builds the foundation of a building
16 appraises a property and writes a report

acquisitions manager ▢ ▢

Words you need

conveyancing Eigentumsübertragung
to draw up (contracts) (Verträge) aufsetzen
foundation Fundament
lease renewal Mietvertragsverlängerung/ -erneuerung
requirement Bedingung
vacant leer stehend
viability Rentabilität

FAQ: Appraisals

What is an appraisal?

A real estate appraisal is an opinion of a property's value. Appraisals are done by certified professional appraisers.

When is an appraisal needed?

An appraisal can be required for a range of purposes such as acquisitions and disposals – that is, whenever real estate is purchased or sold – or in order to secure a loan for financing or to secure a mortgage. Appraisals may also be required for feasibility studies or tax, accounting, and insurance purposes.

The property may be a development or an existing building and could involve any type of use, such as a residential, commercial, or mixed-use scheme.

How is an appraisal done?

The appraiser collects all relevant facts, statistics, and other information regarding the property. The appraiser must research the appropriate markets and all aspects related to the property's value. Based on this information, the appraiser prepares a report that outlines and presents his/her opinion of the property's value.

What qualifications and skills must appraisers have?

In the US, an official license is required to work as an appraiser. A board of appraisers gives certification based on successful completion of a written exam. In the UK, the profession is known as a valuer or valuation surveyor and he or she is normally required to be a member of the Royal Institution of Chartered Surveyors. In addition to a good understanding of appraisal methods, the work requires the ability to write accurate reports, meet deadlines, and communicate well with clients.

"What is a cynic? A man who knows the price of everything, and the value of nothing."
Oscar Wilde

Words you need

existing building Bestandsimmobilie
feasibility study Machbarkeitsstudie
mortgage Hypothek
type of use Nutzungsart

Over to you

- What qualifications are necessary in your country to work as an appraiser?
- Could a valuer from the UK or an appraiser from the US practice in your country?
- Can you list the contents of an appraisal report?
- How frequently are appraisal reports updated?

In this unit you will ...
- review different types of property
- practice saying measurements
- review vocabulary for describing property

3 Viewing the Property

Answer the questions. Then interview your partner to find out his/her answers.

	You	Your Partner
1 Do you think viewing a property is essential?	....	....
2 What types of properties do you view for your work?	....	....
3 How long do you typically spend viewing a property?	....	....
4 What qualities do you look for when viewing a property?	....	....
5 What red flags do you look for?	....	....

1 **Match the pictures with the words in the box.**

apartment building · business park · single-family house (AE) / detached house (BE) · office tower · townhouse (AE) / terraced house (BE) · warehouse

2 **Match the statements (1–5) with the type of property (a–e).**

1 Good management skills and knowledge of the travel industry are essential for this type of real estate.
2 This type of property is used for various purposes, such as e-commerce fulfillment, storage, and distribution.
3 Demographics, disposable income, and foot traffic are important factors for this type of property.
4 Typical occupants of this type of property are finance, insurance, and technology companies.
5 This type of real estate relates to the purchase and renting of everything from country cottages to city apartments.

a office
b warehouse
c retail
d hotel
e residential

3 Read the market report for a central business district (CBD) and fill in the gaps with words from the box.

completion · grades · insurance · location

Supply Low levels of new development will result in a limited supply of property entering the market over the next four years. Refurbished stock will dominate with 78,500 sq m due for ....[1] in the coming year.

Take-up Demand for space in the CBD remained strong during the last 12 months, with take-up amounting to 150,420 sq m. Finance and ....[2] were the dominant sectors among leased properties (>500 sq m), occupying 32 % of the stock.

Vacancy Premium sector vacancies are expected to decline further over the next year and will reach the lowest vacancy rate of all quality ....[3].

Prime Rents Annual prime rents ranged between £420 per sq m and £720 per sq m, depending on building quality and ....[4]. Average annual prime rental growth was positive at 5.0 %, and the average prime achievable rent was £640 per sq m per year.

Words you need

take-up Flächenumsatz
to decline zurückgehen
to range between sich bewegen zwischen
refurbished saniert
stock bestehende (Miet-)Fläche

In the UK, demand is normally measured in "take-up" (Flächenumsatz). In other countries, such as the US and Australia, it's more common to measure demand in "net absorption" (Nettoabsorption).

4 Now match the market report categories (1–4) with the definitions (a–d).

1 Supply
2 Take-up
3 Vacancy
4 Prime Rents

a The highest rent in top locations for top-quality buildings with top-quality amenities.
b The measure of change in occupied stock.
c The sum of all the office space on offer which is not occupied.
d The sum of all the office space on offer, including completions in the next twelve months.

5 🔈08 **Listen to the conversation between a developer and a potential investor. Then identify the features with the correct number (1–6).**

- ☐ elevator
- ☐ basement
- ☐ lobby
- ☐ parking garage
- ☐ reception desk
- ☐ revolving door

Words you need

basement Untergeschoss
furnace Beheizungsanlage
revolving door Drehtür
roof deck Dachterrasse
sprinkler system Sprinkleranlage

Phrases to use

Describing Property

Describing general location
- The building is right on …
- It's just around the corner.
- The office complex is situated in …
- The retail warehouse is located in …

Describing the layout
- This property comprises/ features/offers …
- The building is equipped with many amenities.

Describing the location of rooms
- Down that hallway is …
- The garage is adjacent to …
- This room leads directly to …
- Their offices are directly off the lobby.

6 **You are a real estate agent, and your partner is a prospective tenant. Show your partner around your office or your company's building using the phrases above. Then switch roles.**

Did you know?

Bedrooms in residential properties
In English, the size of a residential property is described by the number of bedrooms. It's always assumed that there are additional rooms, e.g., a living room, a kitchen, etc. Thus, a "Dreizimmerwohnung" is a "two-bedroom apartment" in English.

Floors
The ground floor is called the "first floor" in the US. Therefore, the European first floor is the second floor in the US, and so on. When working with an American business partner, be sure to check which floor you're talking about!

The words "floor" and "story" are used differently. You should say "I work in a three-story building," and "I work on the third floor". Also, note the BE spelling: storey.

Language Traps

German	English
repräsentativ Für unsere Firma benötigen wir ein *repräsentatives* Büro.	**prestigious** We need a *prestigious* office for our company.
Flur Der *Flur* führt direkt ins Wohnzimmer.	**hall, corridor, hallway** The *hall* leads directly into the living room.
Stock Die Büroräume sind im 5. *Stock*.	**floor** The offices are on the 5th *floor*.
Fabrik Wir wollen eine alte *Fabrik* zu einem Bürohaus umgestalten.	**factory, plant** We want to convert an old *factory* into an office building.
Stoff, Material, Bausubstanz Die *Bausubstanz* ist in gutem Zustand.	**fabric** The *fabric* of the building is in good condition.

7 Choose the correct word.

1 The company owns an old textile **fabric | factory**.
2 Are we on the top **hallway | story** of the building?
3 Law firms and banks often prefer **prestigious | representative** properties.
4 Go straight down the **floor | corridor**. Her office is the last door on the left.

Now fill in the gaps using the words that didn't fit in 1–4.

5 The elevator is at the end of this .... on the right.
6 This apartment is .... of the whole building, as you can see all the standard features here.
7 The fitness center is located on the tenth ....
8 The .... of this building is excellent, despite its age.

8 Match the features (1–6) with the definitions (a–f).

1 column
2 open-plan office
3 loading dock
4 raised floor
5 signage
6 suspended ceiling

a platform for loading and unloading trucks
b a large room with many work spaces
c acoustic or cosmetic panels hanging from above
d elevated structure inside a building to hide data and electricity cables, etc.
e part of the building that provides structural support
f exterior structure displaying information or the company logo

Now identify the features with the correct number (1–11).

☐ CCTV • ☐ loading dock • ☐ perimeter fence • ☐ rear/back entrance • ☐ roll-up doors (AE) / roller shutter doors (BE)

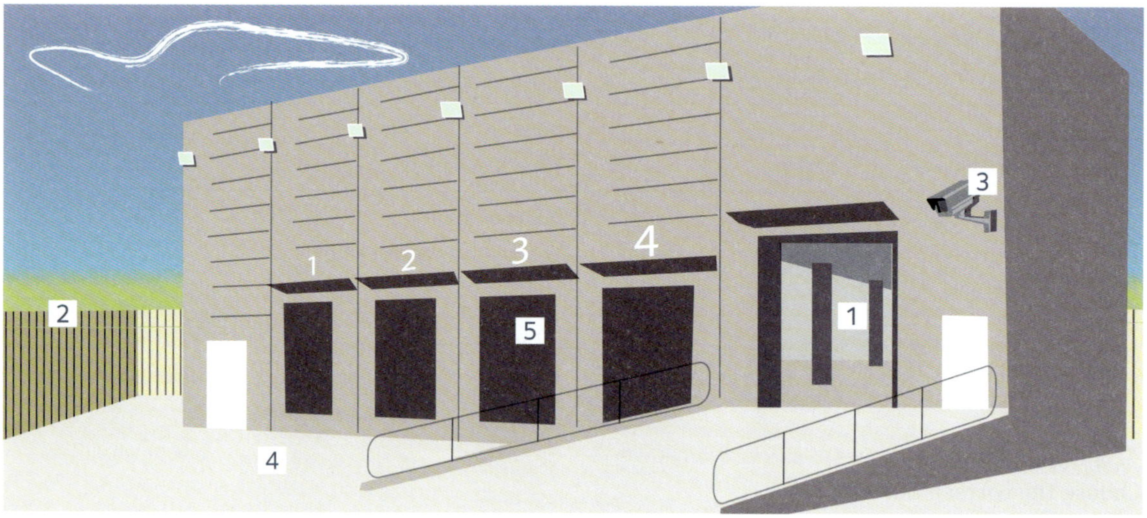

☐ cellular office • ☐ external sun shading • ☐ open-plan office • ☐ reception/lobby • ☐ signage • ☐ suspended ceiling

9 09 **Listen to the dialogue and tick the features that are mentioned.**

- ☐ CCTV
- ☐ clear height
- ☐ columns
- ☐ floor load capacity
- ☐ landscaping
- ☐ net internal area
- ☐ office space
- ☐ parking
- ☐ perimeter fence
- ☐ racks
- ☐ refurbishment
- ☐ roll-up doors
- ☐ signage

Words you need

clear height lichte Höhe
high-bay warehouse Hochregallager
racks Regale

10 09 **Unjumble the words to make sentences from the dialogue. Then listen again and check your answers.**

1 fence | a | CCTV | as well as | there's | perimeter
2 is | the | located | of | building | the | rear | the | at | site
3 are | doors | in | roll-up | there | total | four
4 clear | meters | height | a | doors | of | the | six | have
5 are | columns | few | there | very

11 **Complete the sentences using words from the box.**

> cellular office · columns · external sun shading · landscaping · open-plan office · pallet racks/bays · perimeter fence · raised floor

1 There is more usable space because the .... are wide apart.

2 Cables can be accessed under the ....

3 The building is surrounded by a secure ....

4 I work in a(n) .... with 20 other colleagues.

5 The site features attractive .... with trees and flower beds.

6 The .... protects you from bright light and solar glare.

7 Inventory is stored on .... in horizontal rows with multiple levels.

8 The department head has a(n) ...., which is more private.

Did you know?

Measurements

In English, the size of residential properties is often described by the number of bedrooms and rarely by the amount of space (in square feet or square meters (AE) / metres (BE)).
In commercial property, the floor space is usually given in square meters (sq m) or square feet (sq ft).
Both sq ft and ft^2 can be used for square feet. However, sq ft is more common.

Saying measurements

10.76 ft^2 – *ten point seven six square feet*
We have built a ten-foot wall (not: ~~ten-feet wall~~).
We often use *by* for dimensions: *5 x 6 x 2* is read *five by six by two.*
We read the division sign (/) as *per: $10,000/week* is read *ten thousand dollars per week.*
The numbers after a decimal point are read as single digits, e. g., *2.563* is read *two point five six three.*

Converting measurements

1 sq m is equivalent to 10.764 sq ft.
1 sq ft is equivalent to 0.093 sq m.

Remember that punctuation for numbers is different in English: use a comma to separate the thousands and a point to separate the decimal places. E.g., "Our total expenses came to $1,390.50."

12 10 **Read the measurements out loud. Then listen to hear if you said them correctly.**

1 This office building has approximately 15,000 sq ft of leasable area.
2 The clear height is 3.45 m.
3 The usable area is 23,500 sq m.
4 The floor loading is 25 kN/m^2.
5 The size of the container is 3 x 6 x 8 m.

Now listen to the measurements and write them down.

6 ....

7 ....

8 ....

9 ....

10 ....

13 **Match the phrases from the three columns to form sentences.**

1 This property has a lot	a windows	A all main areas.
2 All offices have fully	b of on-site	B for deliveries.
3 As you can see, the exterior	c installed in	C for signage.
4 There are three passenger	d has a lot of possibilities	D on three sides.
5 Air conditioning is	e extends to the main	E one service elevator.
6 We have floor-to-ceiling	f elevators and	F parking.
7 The landscaping	g accessible	G raised floors.
8 There is also	h a back entrance	H road.

14 **Work with a partner to practice asking about and describing a property.**

▷ Partner File 3: Partner A, page 59 / Partner B, page 60

A Translation Guide for Real Estate Professionals

Eleanor Wise
Property Consultant
Santa Monica, California

Have you ever viewed a property and found that in reality it was different from the details you were sent? The language used to describe a property in a positive way can sometimes lead to misunderstandings. Here is a guide to translate some common phrases used by real estate agents.

	Real Estate Speak	**Plain English**
1	offers a great deal of privacy	you have to drive far to meet any human being
2	situated in a quiet cul-de-sac location	nobody will ever find you
3	an inspection of the site is required	we take no responsibility if you're crazy enough to buy this house
4	centrally located	you may want to buy earplugs
5	with a stunning view of the countryside	hope your car has a strong engine
6	with great potential for conversion	totally run-down, needs fixing, hope you have the money
7	situated within walking distance from the station	if you love one-hour walks
8	wonderful accommodation suited for a single person	extremely small
9	a sought-after residential estate	you are the first who is interested
10	an extraordinary historic building	you need to be a millionaire to restore it
11	with all modern conveniences	we left an oven and an old dishwasher there to make it look like a kitchen
12	on a major road	get used to the smell of car exhaust
13	beautiful landscaping	hope you like extra work
14	plenty of nice shady trees	dark and gloomy
15	the property has been newly refurbished	we want twice what the property is worth

Words you need

cul-de-sac Sackgasse
earplugs Ohrstöpsel
exhaust Abgas
extraordinary außergewöhnlich
gloomy düster
human being Mensch
privacy Privatsphäre
to restore wiederherstellen
sought-after begehrt, gefragt
stunning überwältigend

Over to you

- Have you ever viewed a property and found it was different from the details you were sent?
- In your experience, what features of a property are most often exaggerated?
- What risks are involved when there are inaccuracies or misunderstandings?

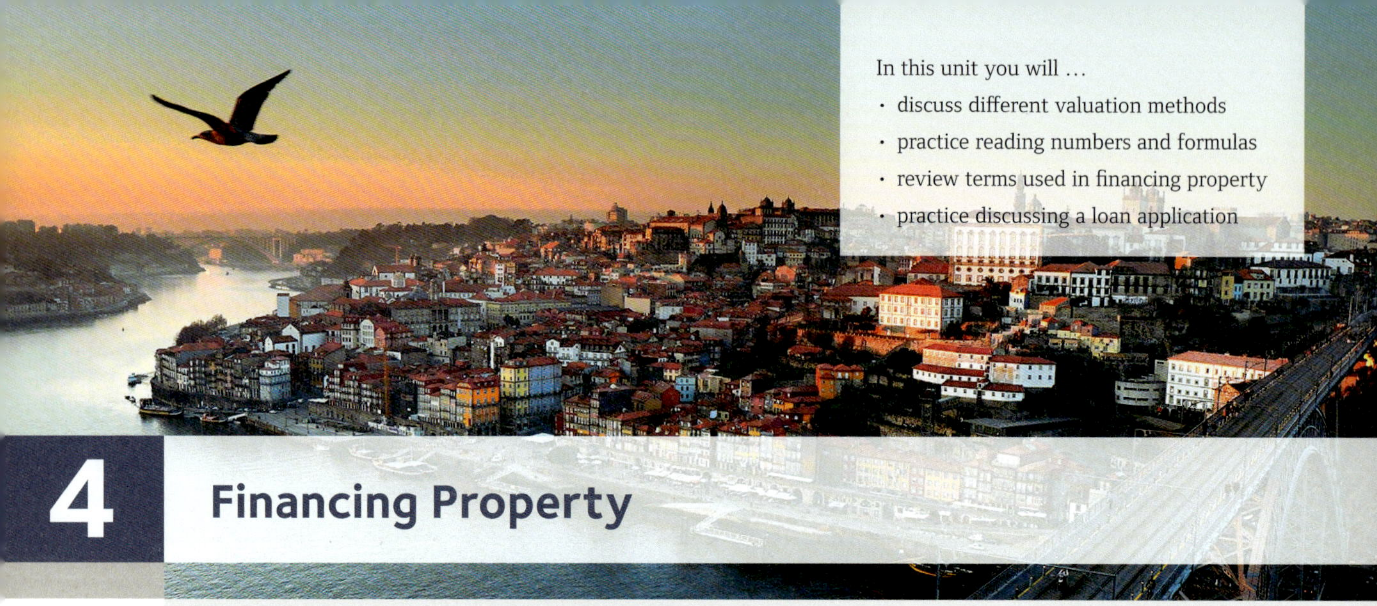

4 Financing Property

In this unit you will …
- discuss different valuation methods
- practice reading numbers and formulas
- review terms used in financing property
- practice discussing a loan application

Below are five steps for financing a property. Put them in the order in which they normally occur, and then compare your answers with your partner's.

- ☐ Lender arranges an appraisal of the property, and an application is prepared for the internal credit committee.
- ☐ Borrower makes contact with the lender, e.g., a bank or independent investment company.
- ☐ Following approval by the lender, loan and security documents are prepared, and the loan is paid out.
- ☐ Borrower and lender negotiate key items of the term sheet, e.g., total amount to be financed (equity ratio), interest rate, loan term, and covenants.
- ☐ Borrower compiles documents, e.g., the business plan and the articles of association.

1 Read the email and decide whether the statements are true or false.

From: Andreas Wulf
To: Beth Ann O'Connell
Subject: Development valuation

Dear Beth Ann,

As you may know, TGM Bank has been looking for new clients in Eastern Europe. As part of this initiative, I'm going to meet Glen Woodrow from NewShare Developments next Tuesday. They've recently set up a Czech subsidiary, and now they're looking for project financing to develop a shopping center on the outskirts of Prague with an investment volume of € 50 million.

30 % of the development has been pre-leased to a major supermarket as an anchor tenant. Currently, we're putting together an application to send to TGM's credit committee for consideration, and we're researching NewShare's financial strength and track record. For this, we'll need to submit an independent valuation of the development.

Since you have experience doing real estate analysis in Eastern Europe, we thought your company would be the ideal partner to undertake this valuation. If you would be available to take this on in the next few weeks, let me know, and also please send details of the valuation methods you would use.

Kind regards,
Andreas

Words you need

anchor tenant Ankermieter
consideration Abwägung, Prüfung
financial strength Bonität
subsidiary Tochterunternehmen
track record Erfolgsbilanz
valuation Bewertung

	True	False
1 Beth Ann is new to the field of real estate valuation.		
2 NewShare is the parent company of a Czech subsidiary.		
3 Andreas needs the valuation to be completed by next week.		
4 Glen is interested in investing in Andreas' company.		
5 The final decision on any investment will be made by Andreas.		

2 **Read the report on common valuation methods, and choose the most appropriate words in blue.**

Real Estate Valuation: A Report on Methods

The methods for real estate valuation can be similar in different countries. The following are methods frequently used in the UK.

The comparative method

We analyze the **insurance | price | height** paid for any comparable property. However, we take into account any differences in size, location, or time of sale. We then use this analysis as a **basics | ground | basis** for estimating the market value of the property.

Discounted cash flow (DCF)

This method evaluates an investment by estimating the **income | price | products** that the property will generate in the future and converting it back to the present, i.e., today's value of money. This process is known as discounting because the **value | worth | fee** of money is calculated back to the present-day value.

The residual method

This method is used for valuing property with development or redevelopment **luck | potential | chance**. The final value of the development is estimated, and all the possible costs such as construction and the profit that the developer expects to make are deducted. The remaining amount is known as the residue, and this is the market value of the **sight | site | place** or property in its condition today.

Words you need

remaining restlich, verbleibend
residue Restwert
to take into account berücksichtigen

3 11 **Listen to the conversation and take notes on the meeting.**

Company: *NewShare Developments*
Type of property: ______
Location: ______
Investment volume: ______
Equity: ______
Tenants: ______
Previous developments: ______
Collateral: ______

4 Circle the correct definition and place the letter in the boxes to form a word which is often used in real estate financing.

1 equity
M Profit made from a real estate investment
E Money borrowed from a bank
T Capital provided by the owners

2 collateral
E Something used as security on a loan
Q Another word for loan agreement
K The initial payment made toward a loan

3 leverage effect
W Only using your own equity
U Borrowing money from a bank
N The increased profit gained by using borrowed money to take advantage of low interest rates

4 anchor tenant
I Shops that sell sailing equipment
A A major shop in a shopping center that is a magnet for other stores
E A shop with a long-term lease

5 negotiations
T Asking someone to help you
R Giving somebody approval to start a project
N To reach an agreement through compromise and discussion

6 pre-lease
T To enter into a lease agreement before the building is completed
B To pay for a service beforehand
Y A lease-free period given as an incentive

☐ ☐ ☐ ☐ ☐ ☐

Words you need

leverage Hebelwirkung
to take advantage of sth. Vorteil aus etw. ziehen

Did you know?

How to read numbers and formulas
4 + 2 = 6 four plus two equals six
10 – 2 = 8 ten minus two equals eight
4 x 4 = 16 four times (or multiplied by) four equals sixteen
12 ÷ 4 = 3 twelve divided by four equals three
20 % twenty percent

In English we use a point (.) and not a comma (,) for decimals
1.1 one point one
3.567 three point five six seven (numbers are read out separately after the decimal point)
0.45 zero (or naught) point four five

Commas are used for figures only when writing thousands
1,284 one thousand two hundred and eighty-four
1,000,000 one million
1,000,000,000 one billion

5 12 **Read out the formulas and numbers. Listen to check your answers.**

1 1.43 %
2 54 ÷ 6 = 9
3 250,625
4 1,543,712
5 € 1,250.45
6 1,435,000 – 233,000 = 1,202,000
7 annual return x 100 / purchase price = gross yield
8 0.3 % of £ 2.5 million

6 13 **Andreas is reading the cash flow statement for Glen's proposed development. Listen and correct the mistakes in the table.**

Cash Flow Statement			
Year	Cash Flow	Discount Factor 10 % (present value of € 1 at 10 %)	Present Value
1	€ 20,000	0.908	€ 18,180
2	€ 40,000	0.836	€ 33,050
3	€ 44,000	0.751	€ 33,044
4	€ 22,000	0.683	€ 15,026
			€ 99,920
		Less outlay	€ 88,000
		New present value	**€ 11,280**

Words you need

cash flow Cashflow/Geldfluss
discount factor Abzinsungsfaktor
less outlay abzüglich Auslagen
present value Barwert

7 **Match the terms with their definitions.**

1 assets
2 balance sheet
3 cash flow
4 collateral
5 credit standing
6 liquidity
7 profit and loss statement
8 track record

a money that moves into and out of a company
b statement of assets and liabilities
c money or property which is provided as security to the lender, e.g., real estate, life insurance, guarantees, etc.
d a person's or company's previous performance or accomplishments
e the ability of an asset to be converted into cash quickly
f a record of a company's ability to meet financial obligations
g something of value, e.g., machinery, cash, buildings, etc.
h a company document showing earnings, expenses and net profits over a period of time

Words you need

accomplishments Leistungen
assets and liabilities Aktiva und Passiva

8 Use the terms in the box to complete the questions.

assets · balance sheet · cash flow · collateral · credit standing · liquidity · profit and loss statement · ~~track record~~

1 Does your management team have a proven *track record* in completing projects on budget?

2 Have your accountants prepared a ………………… and a …………………?

3 What ………………… can be offered as ………………… for borrowing?

4 Is there sufficient ………………… available to meet immediate needs?

5 We need to assess your …………………. Can you provide us with any financial reporting?

6 What is the estimated rental income? We need to undertake a ………………… analysis to help us understand the company's future performance and its ability to service the debt.

Language Traps

German	English
Kredit Wir können Ihnen einen *Kredit* über € 20.000 gewähren.	**loan** We can grant you a *loan* of € 20,000.
Guthaben, im Plus Ihr Konto ist *im Plus*.	**credit** Your account is in *credit*.
Muttergesellschaft, Tochterunternehmen Unsere *Muttergesellschaft* hat ein weiteres *Tochterunternehmen* in Rumänien gegründet.	**parent company, subsidiary** Our *parent company* has set up another *subsidiary* in Romania.
Rate Wir können die monatlichen *Raten* herabsetzen.	**installment** We can reduce the monthly *installments*.
jemandem etwas leihen Ich habe meinem Kollegen etwas Geld *geliehen*.	**to lend something to someone** I *lent* some money to my colleague.
etwas (aus)leihen Kann ich mir kurz Ihren Stift *(aus)leihen*?	**to borrow something** Could I *borrow* your pen for a moment?
Branche Ich arbeite seit zwanzig Jahren in der *Baubranche*.	**business, industry, sector** I have been working in the construction *business* for 20 years.
Filiale Unsere Bank hat eine *Filiale* im Stadtzentrum.	**branch** Our bank has a *branch* in the city center.

Note the difference between "in credit" (im Plus), which is used to describe an account with money in it, and "on credit" (auf Ziel), which is used to describe a method of purchase – e.g., "I bought my car on credit."

9 **Translate the sentences into English.**

1 Wir haben monatliche Ratenzahlungen vereinbart.
2 Kannst du mir dein Wörterbuch bis morgen leihen?
3 Wir müssen uns mehr Kapital borgen, um dieses Projekt zu finanzieren.
4 Ich habe in der Immobilienbranche angefangen.
5 Online-Banking hat zu Schließungen vieler Bankfilialen geführt.

10 **Read the text, then complete the sentences (1–7) using the correct form of the highlighted verbs.**

We're a medium-sized property development company and wanted to take out a loan to buy a greenfield site in order to build a condominium complex. We applied to our bank, and hoped to make an agreement in which they would reschedule the loan if we ran into temporary financial difficulties. Obviously, this required a lot of paperwork, and we hired a consultant to help us prepare the application.

We got a response a week after submitting the application, and it wasn't good. They refused to grant us the loan. They had doubts about our business plan and said we would not be able to repay the full amount. They believed we would default on the loan, i.e., not be able to pay our monthly installments. When that happens, the bank has to call in the loan, i.e., ask the borrower to pay back all the money at once.

They also told us we did not have enough collateral to secure the loan. We've decided to put the project on hold for now. Given the current economic climate, maybe it's for the best.

1 We don't have enough equity. We need to .... a loan.

2 We need to .... your loan by using your home as collateral.

3 The company must .... the loan in installments.

4 The bank will probably .... us the loan because we cannot offer enough collateral.

5 I'm afraid we need to .... the loan because our financial situation has changed.

6 Our client is going through financial difficulties. We hope he will not .... the loan.

7 If we don't have the money to pay our monthly installments, the bank will .... the loan.

11 14 **Listen to the presentation and put the terms in the order in which they are discussed.**

- ☐ Articles of association
- ☐ Arrangement fee
- 1 Borrower
- ☐ Collateral
- ☐ Loan-to-value ratio
- ☐ Maturity

Words you need

arrangement fee Bearbeitungsgebühr
articles of association Gesellschaftsvertrag
extension Verlängerung der Laufzeit
foreclosure Zwangsvollstreckung
loan-to-value ratio (LTV) Beleihungsquote
maturity Fälligkeit
to repossess in Besitz nehmen
term Dauer

Now listen to the extract again and match the sentence parts.

1 The borrower is
2 We've agreed to a 10-year maturity on the loan, but
3 It's quite common to get loans at a loan-to-value ratio of
4 We will require documents such as the
5 In the event of default
6 The arrangement fee is 0.15% of the total loan amount and

a a subsidiary of NewShare Developments.
b articles of association and a company registration certificate.
c is payable upfront, i.e., at the beginning of the loan period.
d the bank may repossess the property or other assets which were offered as collateral.
e 60%, but for investments like this, the percentage is higher.
f the borrower may request a five-year extension.

12 **Work with a partner to practice providing information for a loan application.**

▷ Partner File 4: Partner A, page 59 / Partner B, page 61

Halden, Cristobel & Partners

Home | FAQ | Contact

Interested in acquiring commercial property in the UK? If so, there are a number of issues that you'll have to consider. Here are some frequently asked questions (FAQs) to help you learn more.

HOW IS PROPERTY HELD IN THE UK?

In the UK, you usually deal with a freehold or leasehold property. The owner of a freehold controls and owns the entire property: the land, the buildings and structures on the land, the subsoil below and the airspace above it. A freehold property is effectively absolute ownership and is not limited by time. With a leasehold, one buys the right to occupy land or a building for a given length of time. For example, much of central London (retail, residential, and office) is held on a leasehold basis, the land being owned by the monarchy, the church, or family estates.

DO OTHER TYPES OF REAL ESTATE INTERESTS EXIST IN THE UK?

Yes. These include options (rights to buy or rights of first refusal) and easements (rights to access or use another person's property, such as rights of way and utilities easements).

HOW SHOULD I STRUCTURE MY PROPERTY INVESTMENT?

UK property can be held in a number of different ways, either directly or indirectly. Some of the most common ways to purchase commercial property in the UK are through a limited liability company (LLC), a partnership, or a unit trust. When choosing how to structure the investment, one needs to take into consideration the tax and legal implications.

DO I NEED TO MAKE ANY ENVIRONMENTAL CHECKS?

Yes. After you acquire the property, environmental laws could hold you liable for any contamination already present. Potential environmental risk should be investigated.

DOES THE VENDOR HAVE THE OBLIGATION TO INFORM ME ABOUT DEFECTS AND RESTRICTIONS?

Thorough due diligence is essential, as the vendor may not have disclosed some information such as water damage or contamination. It is also vital that you check whether there are any restrictions which may affect the use of the property.

WHAT ARE THE ACQUISITION FEES?

There are numerous costs associated with the acquisition of property in addition to the purchase price. These are the fees one should expect to pay:

- Agent's fees.
- Valuation/survey fees.
- Legal fees. Normally a percentage of the purchase price plus value-added tax (VAT). Costs depend on the nature of the transaction.
- Transfer tax (known in the UK as stamp duty land tax).
- Finance costs. Arrangement fee and the fees charged by your bank's lawyers and valuers.
- Other professional costs. Non-UK companies may need a letter from a lawyer confirming they have the financial capacity to enter into the property transaction.

Words you need

contamination Altlast(en)
easement Grunddienstbarkeit
freehold Grundeigentum
leasehold Erbaurecht
limited liability company (LLC) GmbH
right of first refusal Vorkaufsrecht
right of way Wegerecht
subsoil Untergrund
value-added tax (VAT) Mehrwertsteuer

Over to you

- Do you have any experience purchasing commercial property in the UK? Did you encounter the same fees that are outlined above?
- How does purchasing commercial property in the UK compare with your country?
- What types of easements have you come across? How do easements and rights of first refusal affect property transactions in your country?

In this unit you will …
- practice the language of buying and selling real estate
- read about due diligence and letters of intent
- review the terminology of leasing
- practice conditionals and the language of negotiation

5 Buying, Selling, and Leasing

Match the topics to the statements.

☐ due diligence ☐ letter of intent ☐ negotiation ☐ tenant agreement

1 The seller will be informed in writing that we are serious about buying this property and will be asked not to search for any other potential buyers for the moment.

2 We also need to check all the details and verify that this is a solid investment. Our engineers will have a closer look at the building, our property lawyers will look at the contracts, and the real estate agents will look at the commercial side.

3 We will need to find retailers and restaurants to lease space in our building. We have to make sure that the rent they pay reflects the quality of the location.

4 After weeks of discussions, we are very close to reaching an agreement on the purchase price.

1 **The flow chart shows the steps taken in a sales transaction. Fill in the gaps by matching the verbs with the nouns to make word pairs.**

enter into · hand over · negotiate · receive · sign · submit · undertake · view

a .... property
↓
b .... letter of intent (LOI)
↓
c .... due diligence
→
d .... board approval
↑
e .... purchase agreement
→
f .... contract
↓
g .... property
↓
h .... registry of deeds

Would it be possible to do any of the steps in a different order? Discuss with a partner.

Did you know?

Lease, Let, and Rent

The verbs *to lease* (AE) and *to let* (BE) both mean *vermieten*. The owner who leases property to tenants is called the *landlord (Vermieter)*.

The owner has leased the offices to a small law firm.

The landlord has decided to let the entire floor to an IT company.

The verb *to rent* can mean both *mieten* and *vermieten*. When *to rent* means *vermieten*, the preposition *out* is sometimes added to indicate this meaning. The verb *to rent* is usually used in a less formal context.

My neighbor sometimes rents (out) her apartment to students.

Our company has expanded and we need to rent a larger office.

The noun *rent (Miete)* describes the amount of money paid or received for leased property.

In San Francisco, the average rent for a retail space has increased significantly.

The noun *lease (Mietvertrag)* refers to the written legal agreement between the owner and the tenant.

In leases, the landlord is often called the *lessor*, and the tenant is often called the *lessee*.

2 **Certain words are frequently used in letters of intent (LOI). Match the words (1–5) with their definitions (a–e).**

1 approval
2 deed of transfer
3 freehold
4 service charges
5 title

a legal document which provides new ownership details
b document showing a person's right of ownership
c maintenance costs that the tenant pays to the owner
d official authorization to do something
e ownership of property without a time limit, i.e., opposite of leasehold

Leasehold property is rare in the US, where almost all ownership is freehold (i.e., ownership without restriction). For more about leasehold and freehold, see the article on page 39.

3 Use the words in the box to complete the LOI.

approval · deed of transfer · freehold · inspection · leasable · parking spaces · party · service charges · terms and conditions · title

RIDGELINE INVESTMENTS

10 Battery Street, Suite 1100 • San Francisco, CA 94111

Dear Mr. Adams,

We would like to thank you for inviting us to consider the sale and purchase of Lichtenberger Straße 140, Berlin.

We have set out below the terms under which Ridgeline Investments would be interested in acquiring the property. We have based our considerations on the information provided in your investment memorandum as well as an external visual ....[1] of the property on August 2. Formal ....[2] from the board of directors will depend on the satisfactory completion of due diligence and valuation.

1. The Seller
We understand that XLM Consolidated Properties is the seller (the "Seller").

2. The Purchaser
The building would be purchased by Ridgeline Investments (the "Purchaser").

3. The Building

We understand that the building is to be sold as a ....[3], free of debt, liens, and encumbrances. The building includes approximately 12,000 sq m of ....[4] area and 60 ....[5].

4. Purchase Price
We will work towards a sale and purchase agreement and will proceed with our due diligence based on a non-binding price of

EUR 40,000,000.-
(forty million Euros)
(the "Purchase Price")

We have calculated the Purchase Price on the basis of an assumed fully indexed rental income for the building of € 2,040,000 per annum, VAT, and ....[6], for a period until 2017. This reflects a gross initial yield of 5.1 %.

The Purchase Price will be payable in full upon transfer of the ....[7] and handover of the building and is subject to the ....[8] set out in this letter being incorporated into the binding agreement. The costs incurred for the transfer of ownership, including the costs of drawing up the contract of sale and the ....[9] will be at the Purchaser's expense. Each ....[10] will bear the costs of their own advisers.

5. Conditions

The word "seller" is often used in America for the person who sells real estate. In the United Kingdom, the word "vendor" is also used.

Words you need

assumed angenommen
binding (rechtlich) bindend
costs incurred angefallene Kosten
encumbrance Grundstücksbelastung
lien Grundpfandrecht

4 **Find the words or phrases in the LOI that correspond to the German terms.**

1 .... *Kosten tragen*

2 .... *Mieteinnahmen*

3 .... *einen Vertrag aufsetzen*

4 .... *unterliegt den Geschäftsbedingungen*

5 .... *verbindliche Vereinbarung*

5 15 **Listen to a description of the due diligence process and mark the statements as true or false.**

	True	False
1 The due diligence period is rarely short.		
2 Technical specialists determine if hazardous materials have been used.		
3 Lawyers verify compliance with building regulations.		
4 An acquisitions manager may undertake the commercial due diligence.		
5 The final sale price must be agreed to before the due diligence process.		

6 15 **Fill in the missing words to complete phrases from the audio. Listen again to check.**

1 construction ....

2 .... installations

3 state of ....

4 .... materials

5 title ....

6 building ....

7 rights ....

8 restrictive ....

9 credit ....

10 market ....

Which of these elements are legal (L), business (B), or technical (T)? Write the appropriate letter in the box next to each phrase.

Did you know?

The word *covenant* can have different meanings.
In real estate, a good covenant is often used to describe a tenant with a good credit standing *(Bonität).*

The credit rating agency is assessing the tenant's covenant strength.

Covenant can also be used to describe a mutual agreement. This could mean a contract *(Vertrag)* or it can refer to a specific clause or terms in a contract *(Vertragsklausel).*

The borrower has agreed to the covenants required by the lender.

A restrictive covenant on land *(Nutzungsbeschränkung)* can also be found in the registry of deeds (AE) / Land Registry (BE).

The restrictive covenant states that it is not possible to trade on the property.

7 Read the email and answer the questions.

From: lbausch@sinton-associates.com
To: robert.finch@lkww.com
Subject: Common terms for tenancy agreements

Hello Rob,

At our meeting yesterday you asked me to send you some information on tenancy agreement terminology. Here are some of the most common terms.

Rent
In Central Europe we often talk about rent levels on a monthly basis, e.g., "the rent is €34 per sq m". In the UK and America, rent for commercial property is usually described on an annual basis, e.g., "the rent is $320 per sq m".

Indexation
The US and Germany have similar systems for increasing rent. In the US this is known as *escalation* and is related to the consumer price index (CPI) with an escalator clause.

In the UK, rent is normally adjusted every five years depending on the rental value. This is known as a *rent review* and is either negotiated or detailed in the tenancy agreement. Rent reviews are normally upward only, which means the cost can only increase during rent review negotiations.

Terms of lease
The lease (also known as a tenancy agreement) often has standard terms in English depending on what costs have been negotiated with the tenant. A net lease requires the tenant to pay some or all of the property expenses in addition to the fixed rent.

Single net lease: the tenant is responsible for paying property taxes as well as the fixed rent.

Double net lease: the tenant pays all property taxes and insurance expenses as well as the fixed rent. This can be comparable to *Dach und Fach* in German-speaking countries.

Triple net lease: in addition to the fixed rent, the tenant agrees to pay all property taxes, insurance, maintenance, and repairs to the structural building elements. In English, this is also known as a *full repairing and insuring lease*. A triple net lease is often negotiated with tenants for institutional properties.

Hope this helps. Give me a call if you have any more questions.

Best wishes,

Laura

1 How do the descriptions of rent differ in Germany and the UK?
2 How is rent increased in the UK?
3 What differences can lease contracts have?
4 What other term can be used for a *full repairing and insuring lease*?
5 What is an *escalation*?

Negotiations (I)

Expressing agreement
- That sounds fine.
- Yes, I think we can accept that.
- I'd be willing to … provided that …
- That seems perfectly reasonable to me.
- I have no objections to that.
- Yes, I am happy/satisfied with that.

Expressing partial agreement
- I tend to agree with you, but …
- I see what you're saying, but ...
- That might be true. However, …

Expressing disagreement
- I'm afraid we can't accept that.
- I'm afraid that is out of the question for us.
- Unfortunately, we don't see eye to eye on that.

Clarifying
- We really must clarify this issue.
- So, if I understand you correctly, …
- Could you expand on that?

8 16 **Listen to the dialogue and tick the phrases that are used.**

1 Could you expand on that? ☐
2 We really must clarify this issue. ☐
3 I have no objections to that. ☐
4 You may have a point about … ☐
5 I'm not sure I can agree to that. ☐
6 I think I can agree to that. ☐
7 That seems perfectly reasonable to me. ☐

Listen again and complete the sentences.

There are a number of ……………… [1] we need to discuss before we can negotiate the purchase agreement.

What would you ……………… [2]?

If we ……………… [3] the repair costs from the purchase price, we could come to a(n) ……………… [4] on this point.

I think we can do that, on the ……………… [5] that we have a(n) ……………… [6] in the agreement which details this issue.

Well, I think I can ……………… [7] to that.

Negotiations (II)

Offering a compromise

- We are prepared to offer … if you …
- We are ready to … on the understanding that …
- We are happy to offer/give you … if …
- We can accept that, provided …
- I'm willing to … , provided that … / as long as …

Expressing conditions

When we talk about what will happen or is likely to happen in the future, we use

- If + present tense form, (then) will + verb

*If you **pay** the full rent by the end of the month, you **will avoid** any additional fees.*

When we describe a hypothetical situation, we use

- If + past tense form, (then) would + verb

*If our location **was/were** more central, we **would attract** more business.*

In conditional sentences, you can also put the *if*-clause at the end.

*We **will give** you a 3 % rent reduction if you **sign** the lease today.*

*They **would move** to a larger office if they **had** more employees.*

Can, may, could, and *might* can often be used instead of *will* and *would*.

9 Complete the *if*-sentences below.

1 If we ………… (own) more land, we ………… (build) another warehouse.

2 If the clients ………… (accept) our offer tomorrow, we ………… (sign) the contract.

3 We ………… (consider) your offer if the building ………… (have) more square footage.

4 If we ………… (have) more investors, we ………… (pursue) this opportunity.

5 I ………… (accept) the offer if I ………… (be) you.

10 Rephrase the sentences using *if*.

1 You must lower your fee. Then I will accept the broker conditions.

If you lower the fee, I will accept the broker conditions.

2 We can accept the purchase price, but you must decontaminate the site.

If …………

3 We'll approve your application for a conversion, but you must get approval from a structural engineer first.

If …………

4 I don't have € 5 million, but I want to buy a villa in Munich.

If …………

5 You don't have an anchor tenant. That's why we won't invest.

If …………

6 We're prepared to finance the project, but you must provide more collateral.

If …………

11 Work with a partner to practice negotiating the terms of a purchase agreement.

▷ Partner File 5: Partner A, page 59 / Partner B, page 61

12 **Replace the highlighted phrases in the purchase agreement with the words in the box.**

burdens · from · guarantees · in accordance with · inform · legal right of ownership · paid

PURCHASE AGREEMENT

by and between XLM Consolidated Properties, a limited liability company (Seller), and Ridgeline Investments (Purchaser).

The Seller hereby agrees to sell and convey to the Purchaser and the Purchaser hereby agrees to purchase from the Seller, subject to[1] the terms and conditions hereinafter set forth.

The parties agree to and apply for registration of a priority notice in the registry of deeds in order to secure the Purchaser's claim to title[2] to the property.

The property shall be transferred free from any encumbrances[3] registered in sections II and III of the registry of deeds. It is hereby agreed to have the mortgage entry removed from section III of the registry of deeds.

The Seller hereby authorizes the Purchaser to enjoy the benefit of all rights and to bear all obligations resulting from the lease as of[4] the date of the passing of possession, i.e., before the transfer of title.

The Seller warrants[5] that they are not aware of any substantial defects in the building. The Purchaser has had the property examined and inspected by experts and is, therefore, aware of the conditions of the property.

The Seller shall notify[6] the Purchaser in writing and without delay of any facts which would influence the warranties of this Agreement.

The costs arising from setting up this agreement shall be borne[7] by the Purchaser.

Words you need

to enjoy the right to do sth. das Recht haben, etw. zu tun
hereinafter im Folgenden
priority notice Auflassungsvormerkung
to secure schützen
set forth wie dargelegt

13 **Decide if the interpretations of the purchase agreement are true or false.**

	True	False
1 XLM Consolidated Properties is a limited liability company.		
2 Ridgeline Investments wants to sell the property to XLM Consolidated Properties.		
3 The Purchaser has undertaken due diligence.		
4 The mortgage entry should be removed from the registry of deeds.		
5 The Purchaser has no right to enter the property before the title has been transferred.		
6 The Seller will cover the costs for drawing up the purchase agreement.		

Did you know?

Note that the word *shall* in legal agreements is a synonym for *must*. "All costs shall be borne by the seller" is translated as *"Alle Kosten werden vom Verkäufer getragen."*

Language Traps

German	English
seriös J & T ist ein *seriöses* Immobilienunternehmen.	**reputable** J & T is a *reputable* real estate company.
ernst(haft) Die Firma meint es mit ihrem Kaufangebot *ernst*.	**serious** The company is *serious* about their bid.
Rendite Wir haben die *Rendite* mit 5% berechnet.	**yield** We have calculated the *yield* as 5%.
rentabel Dieses Geschäft war sehr *rentabel*.	**profitable** This deal has been very *profitable*.
Provision Wir stellen 2% *Provision* in Rechnung.	**commission** We charge 2% *commission*.
Vorschrift Das Gesetz enthält eine *Vorschrift* für internationale Konzerne.	**provision** The law includes a *provision* for international corporations.

14 **Translate the sentences into English.**

1 Der Kunde hat die Provision für dieses Objekt noch nicht gezahlt.
2 Dieses Bürogebäude ist für uns nicht rentabel.
3 Wir wollen eine Rendite von 6% erreichen.
4 „Diese Kaufinteressenten scheinen seriös zu sein." – „Meinst du das ernst?"

Tips for a Transaction That No One Will Forget!

By Tom Roth, Real Estate Consultant

FOR THE BUYER

- **Be unprepared**

If you really know your job, the best thing is to improvise. There's no need to spend valuable time researching the property. If you're negotiating, say, the purchase price of a property, don't worry about all the little details. The seller will be impressed by the fact that you arrive at the appointment without any big folders.

- **Trust and be trusted**

You should always trust everyone. Impress the seller by how courageous you are. Don't ask too many questions about restrictive covenants or any other regulations that might influence the deal. Otherwise, they might think you're questioning their integrity. That's the last thing you want!

FOR THE SELLER

- **Cut the small talk**

Small talk is highly overrated. Hard-nosed businesspeople are past that stage. Don't beat around the bush. Get to the point, because time is money. You want to create an atmosphere that leaves no room for personal chitchat. You'll make the buyer very happy if you don't waste time on small talk before getting down to the nitty-gritty of making deals.

- **Throw in a few surprises**

Why not get more fun out of life? As soon as the buyer enters your office to sign the purchase contract, say that someone else has just offered 10% more. This practice, known as "gazumping ", can scare the living daylights out of people! Then, after you've caused everyone to have a heart attack, say that you really don't want to sell to anyone else because they're so nice.

FOR EVERYONE

- **Always be late**

You should never arrive to a meeting on time. This is the best way to be taken seriously. Your business partner will be terribly impressed and will assume you have many more important things to do. And don't apologize for being late – "just walk in like you own the place," as they say in America.

Words you need

to beat around the bush um den heißen Brei herumreden
courageous mutig
to gazump entgegen vorheriger Zusage das Objekt an einen Höherbietenden verkaufen
hard-nosed abgebrüht
impressed beeindruckt
nitty-gritty wichtigste Punkte
overrated überbewertet
to scare the living daylights out of s.o. jemanden zu Tode erschrecken

Over to you

- What tips would you give to help someone be successful at selling property?
- Based on your experience, why do property negotiations fail?
- Is it always important to maintain a good relationship with your business contacts? Give reasons.
- How do you know you can trust a business partner? What has been your experience?

In this unit you will …
- practice expressions used in property management
- review trade professions
- practice taking messages
- read about service charges

6 Managing Property

Read the list of statements about managing property and decide whether you agree or disagree. Compare your answers with your partner's.

		Agree	Disagree
1	As long as the tenants pay their rent, there is no need to contact them.	☐	☐
2	Managing corporate real estate is about supporting the owner's business needs.	☐	☐
3	Managing property is a complex job involving many different tasks and skills, and to work in this field you have to be an expert in all areas involved.	☐	☐
4	Property managers should be responsible for keeping operating costs low.	☐	☐
5	Managing property is all about keeping the building in a good condition. If the owner wants to increase its value, that is his or her responsibility.	☐	☐

1 **Read the *About Us* page from the website of a property management company.**

Home
About Us
Testimonials
Careers
Contact

Curate Real Estate Management *Your Partner in Managing Property*

At Curate Real Estate Management (CREM), we offer state-of-the-art facility and property management services to help you maintain and add value to your real estate.

We offer a range of services, including lease administration and bookkeeping. In addition, we also procure and manage specialists for maintenance, repairs and refurbishments, compliance with legal requirements, and much more.

We're committed to making sure your property is clean, functional, and secure. We offer advice and assistance in the procurement of the following:

- Security services
- Internal and external cleaning services
- Waste removal
- Pest control
- Landscaping

Now complete the gaps to form words or expressions from the website that match the definitions.

1 _ O _ _ _ I _ _ C _ observance of specific standards or laws

2 _ _ S _   _ _ N T _ _ _ protection from potentially harmful animals and insects such as mice, rats, and cockroaches

3 _ _ O C _ _ E _ E _ _ the process of obtaining the services of contractors, tradespersons, etc.

4 _ A _ _ _ C _ _ I _ _ creation and maintenance of external green areas

2 **Use the words in the box to complete the sentences.**

based · divided · employs · founded · headquarters · portfolio

- Curate Real Estate Management (CREM) was ....[1] in 2009 by its current president and CEO, Lynne Randall. CREM is ....[2] in Vancouver. Our ....[3] are in the downtown area, and we have over twenty branches throughout Canada.
- Our company is ....[4] into two departments that reflect our main service segments: Facility Management and Property Management.
- CREM ....[5] over 120 people who have an impressive track record in the real estate business. Currently, we have a ....[6] of over 11 million sq ft of residential rentals, condominiums, and commercial properties.

Phrases to use

How to present your company

- We have annual sales / an annual turnover of …
- The company was founded/established in …
- The company is based in …
- The company has several branches in …
- The headquarters … is/are in …
- We employ … / The company employs …
- Our company is divided into … departments.
- We have a portfolio of …
- We offer …
- Our services include …

3 **Working with a partner, present your company and describe your position in the company. Then switch roles. Use phrases from the box above.**

4 17 **Now listen to an interview with the CEO of Curate Real Estate Management. Decide if the statements are true or false.**

	True	False
1 There is one universal approach to managing property.		
2 Facility management is completely separate from property management.		
3 In larger organizations, one employee may be responsible for just one area.		
4 The property manager is not often on site.		
5 The facility manager is required to be an electrician and a plumber.		

Words you need

day-to-day (tag)täglich
janitorial services Hausmeisterdienste
on site vor Ort
plumber Klempner/in

Defining Roles: Asset, Property, and Facility Management

The management of commercial and residential properties is a wide-ranging and complex field. There are far too many skills involved for one person to work at all levels of real estate management; on the other hand, there can be some overlap between different areas.

As shown in the diagram, the asset manager is responsible for general strategy with the goal of maximizing the investment of the owners. The property manager is more involved in tenant relations and the daily responsibility of keeping the business side of things organized and functional. The facility manager spends a lot of time on site and has a more hands-on responsibility for operations.

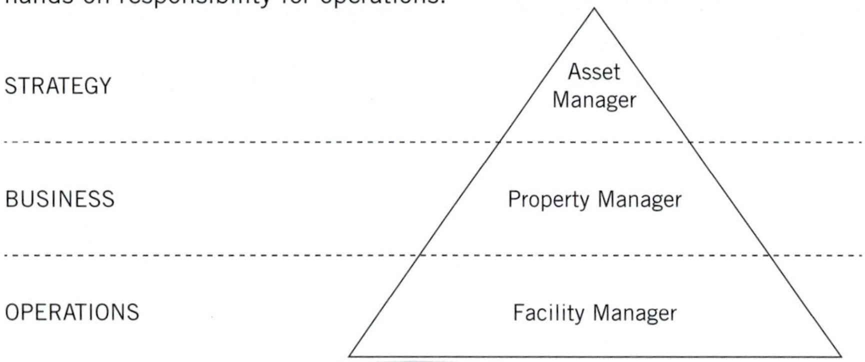

5 Match the verbs (1–6) with the nouns (a–f) to form expressions often used in real estate.

1 oversee	a performance
2 negotiate	b information
3 develop	c budget
4 measure	d contracts
5 hire	e tenant moves
6 provide	f contractors

Now use the expressions to complete the sentences.

1 Asset managers .... a .... to make the most efficient use of the money available.

2 Asset managers .... the .... of real estate assets to achieve maximum value.

3 Property managers .... for the asset manager on matters such as rental income.

4 Property and asset managers .... with tenants, and the final document is usually drawn up by lawyers.

5 Property managers .... to make sure that the handover of the property goes smoothly.

6 Facility managers .... to carry out any necessary maintenance and repair work.

6 Match the tradespeople (A–H) to their tasks (1–8).

1 There are cracks in the wall which need to be filled.
2 A tenant needs additional electrical outlets installed.
3 A water pipe is leaking.
4 A mouse was seen in the stairway.
5 Custom shelving needs to be built.
6 The heating doesn't seem to work.
7 The weeds need to be removed from the flower beds.
8 The corridor needs a new coat of paint.

A painter

B carpenter

C plumber

D building services technician

E exterminator

F plasterer

G electrician

H landscaper

Did you know?

A tradesperson *(Handwerker)* is a skilled worker in a specialized area, e.g., an electrician, plumber, or carpenter. He or she is usually independent or employed by an outside company.

A building superintendent (AE) / caretaker (BE) *(Hausmeister)* has more general skills and takes care of basic maintenance. The superintendent is informally referred to as the "super". He or she is usually employed by the property owner or management company.

Words you need

coat of paint Anstrich
crack Riss
electrical outlet Steckdose
to leak undicht sein
pipe Rohr
shelving Regale
weeds Unkraut

7 18–22 Listen to the voicemail messages and take down notes.

Message 1
Name: ....
To Do: ....
....
....
Phone Number: ....

Message 2
Name: ....
To Do: ....
....
....
Phone Number: ....

Message 3
Name: ....
To Do: ....
....
....
Phone Number: ....

Message 4
Name: ....
To Do: ....
....
....
Phone Number: ....

Message 5
Name: ....
To Do: ....
....
....
Phone Number: ....

8 Work with a partner to practice discussing tenant problems.

▷ Partner File 6: Partner A, page 59 / Partner B, page 61

9 Use the words in the box to complete the email.

accounting · benefit · cleaning · dispute · estimate · maintenance · recovered · tenants

From: jld@crem.ca
To: ilo@crem.ca
Subject: Service Charges

Dear Ian,

It was great to meet you yesterday – welcome to the team! I'm looking forward to working together with you here at CREM.

Following up on our discussion, I'm sending you here a short summary explaining the purpose of service charges and how we calculate them.

Service charges are costs for work such as repair and ....[1] to the property and for the provision of heating, lighting, ...[2], security, etc. The costs of providing the services to a property are ....[3] from the users through these charges. It is important to note that the total costs recovered cannot be increased for profit. However, there should also be no remaining loss left for the owner to pay (at least for a fully leased property).

In buildings occupied by a number of ....[4], the costs are shared. This is called apportionment. A common method of sharing costs is according to the size of the rental space. Services that are only provided to some occupants are divided among only those who ....[5] from those services.

There is a lot of potential for ....[6] between landlords and tenants if the service charges are not managed properly. We therefore provide tenants with a(n) ....[7] of the service charges and an explanation of how they are apportioned in advance. This ensures transparency.

Finally, the payment we receive for a) managing the services listed in the service charges, b) supervising the on-site team, c) overseeing site contractors, and d) doing the ....[8] is known as the management fee.

Should you have any further questions, please don't hesitate to contact me.

Kind regards,
Jacob

10 Now answer the questions about the email.

1 How are service charges defined in the email?
2 How much do service charges add to the owner's profit?
3 What happens to the costs in multi-tenant buildings?
4 How is transparency ensured?

11 Use the words in the box to complete the service charge statement.

Accounting fees • Cleaning • Electricity • Elevators and escalators • Public liability

SERVICE CHARGE STATEMENT
Expenditure summary report for the period January 1 to December 31.

	Total Expenses	Tenant 1
MANAGEMENT		
1 Management fees	$ 50,000	$ 12,500
2	$ 1,800	$ 450
UTILITIES		
3	$ 350,800	$ 110,000
4 Gas	$ 12,080	$ 5,000
5 Heating	$ 13,660	
6 Water and sewage charges	$ 7,200	$ 3,600
SOFT SERVICES		
7 Security	$ 120,200	$ 3,050
8	$ 137,000	$ 3,500
9 Waste management	$ 10,400	$ 2,600
10 Pest control	$ 1,800	$ 450
11 Landscaping	$ 7,000	$ 1,750
HARD SERVICES		
12 Mechanical and Electrical (M&E) services, e.g., repairs	$ 160,200	$ 40,050
13	$ 19,253	$ 4,801
14 Fabric repairs and maintenance	$ 80,000	$ 20,000
INSURANCE		
15 Building (fire, flood, theft)	$ 800	$ 200
16 Building contents	–	–
17	$ 400	$ 100
EXCEPTIONAL EXPENDITURE		
18 Major work, e.g., refurbishment, structural repairs	$ 64,564	–

12 Read the sentences and write the corresponding number from the service charge statement.

1 We need to get rid of ants and rats in the storeroom. ☐
2 All risks are covered by a policy. ☐
3 These staff members make sure uninvited guests cannot enter the building. ☐
4 We want to keep green areas tidy and attractive. ☐
5 According to city regulations, all machinery must be inspected regularly. ☐
6 A new, more efficient heating system will be installed. ☐
7 The façade needs painting and there is water damage in the roof that needs to be fixed. ☐
8 The staff sweep and polish the floors, leaving them free from dirt. ☐
9 The costs of preparing financial documents must be kept low. ☐
10 We employ 13 staff to look after the properties we manage. ☐
11 Our company has decided to change providers. Now our clients pay a little less per kilowatt-hour. ☐
12 We organize regular inspections to make sure that our tenants will never have to walk up the stairs to get to their offices. ☐

Words you need

to apportion (Kosten) umlegen
escalator Rolltreppe
flood Überschwemmung
to get rid of loswerden, entsorgen
provision Bereitstellung
sewage Abwasser
tidy ordentlich
utilities Versorgungseinrichtungen

Language Traps

German	English
kontrollieren Wir haben die Abrechnungen *kontrolliert*.	**check, inspect** We have *checked* the monthly accounts.
steuern, regeln Die Lichttechnik kann zentral *gesteuert* werden.	**control** The lighting can be *controlled* centrally.
Kaution In vielen Ländern muss für ein Mietobjekt eine *Kaution* hinterlegt werden.	**deposit** In many countries a *deposit* has to be paid for leased premises.
Vorsicht Besonders bei Bauprojekten öffentlichen Interesses müssen wir *Vorsicht* walten lassen.	**caution** We need to exercise *caution* with projects of public interest.
ökonomisch, sparsam Wir suchen nach der *sparsamsten* Heiztechnik für dieses Gebäude.	**economical** We are looking for the most *economical* heating technology for this building.
wirtschaftlich, auf die Ökonomie bezogen Die gesamte *wirtschaftliche* Situation des Landes wirkt sich auf den Immobilienmarkt aus.	**economic** The overall *economic* situation affects the real estate market.
Technik Wir haben die Telekommunikations*technik* im gesamten Gebäude modernisiert.	**technology** We have modernized the telecommunications *technology* in the entire building.
Technik (im Sinne von Methode) Ihre Verkaufs*technik* lässt noch zu wünschen übrig.	**technique** Your sales *technique* still leaves a lot to be desired.
isolieren Die Wand ist gut *isoliert*.	**insulate** The wall is well *insulated*.

13 **Correct the mistakes in the sentences.**

1 We have state-of-the-art technique in the office building.
2 Tenants usually pay a caution before they move into their apartments.
3 Our lawyers have controlled all the tenant agreements.
4 Heating with oil is not very economic.
5 The roof is not very well isolated.

Real World Real Estate

Straight from the Source: Here are a few tips from professionals in the field of real estate management.

"Firstly, I try to understand the client's objectives. I consider several variables in the client's portfolio, including the size of the organization, the number and type of assets under management, and their business goals, e.g., current income vs. capital gain. My overall aim is to manage the long-term appreciation of the real estate as well as short-term cash flow and to find the ideal balance between risk and returns, thus increasing the value of the portfolio."
–Stephanie Alexander, Asset Manager

"There has been a change in attitude towards tenants. Treating tenants as customers has become fundamental because they are the main source of income and cash flow for properties. Ultimately, tenants are the key to success for any investment. We can improve our working relationship with them by gaining a good understanding of their business and the sector in which they work. I keep up to date by reading press releases, company reports, and the tenant's website."
–Wendy Galton-Hood, Property Manager

"An important part of my job is to make sure that the property has a low vacancy rate or, ideally, is fully leased. Once a new tenant signs a lease, I can't just put my feet up! Keeping tenants is just as important as finding new ones. I also make sure I keep track of the tenant's financial situation. Running a credit check before the initial lease has been negotiated is only the beginning! If we know about their financial status, we can anticipate possible problems with rent payments. As a result, we can work together to find a solution."
–Eric Walderman, Property Manager

"Ask for feedback. Find out what the tenant thinks about their space, the building, and the way it is managed and what they like or dislike. Knowing this can improve relations with tenants and show investors you are taking an active interest in their investment. Remember, problems that are identified must be dealt with ASAP!"
–Dennis Beasley, Property Manager

Words you need

capital gain Veräußerungsgewinn
to keep track of sth. etw. im Auge behalten
press release Pressenotiz

Over to you

- In your experience, are these views typical for their professions?
- Do you believe that tenants expect too much from their landlords? Explain.
- What is your experience of the relationship between property management and tenants?
- Do you agree that the role of property management has changed? If so, how?

Partner Files

Partner A

Unit 1

Exercise 11 • File 1

▷ p. 12

You are a real estate agent. An independent retailer is looking for a new location for his or her shop. Ask what kind of shop it is, and then answer questions about the following three locations. Make a final recommendation on the best location for the shop and give reasons.

Centennial Harbor
120 sq m
- waterfront property
- 20-minute walk to the city center
- plenty of free parking
- good bus connections to restaurants, bars, and movie theaters
- a supermarket and other shops located nearby
- four-star hotel recently opened in the area

Silicon Park
1,100 sq m
- located in one of the area's major business parks
- retail unit in office building shared with major corporation
- located only eight miles from the city center
- major shopping mall ten minutes away by car
- easy access to highway
- underground parking garage

Station Road
500 sq m
- five-minute walk to the city center
- 15-minute walk to the government district
- three-story parking garage nearby
- bus stop across the street
- small shops and several museums in the area
- mix of restaurants and office space
- shopping mall in the train station (currently under construction)

Unit 2

Exercise 9 • File 2

▷ p. 21

You are a real estate agent. Call a prospective investor to find out his or her investment profile and fill in the form. You currently have two properties that might be of interest. Describe the properties.

Country: ____________________
Property type: ____________________
Investment volume: ____________________
Location factors: ____________________
Other preferences: ____________________
____

Intex Corporate Center (€15 million)
- Situated on the outskirts of Frankfurt, built ten years ago, a few kilometers away from the airport, direct access to several major roads (A5, A3), good public transportation, with individual units that can be leased
- Approx. 8,000 sq m in leasable floor space; office space on three levels (currently leased to a blue-chip IT company for the next five years); 300 sq m of ground-floor retail space; on-site parking lot

Anderberg Business Center (€40 million)
- Logistics center leased to the Austrian Shipping Company (ASC) for the next 10 years, built two years ago, close to the border with the Czech Republic, direct rail connection, one-hour drive to Vienna
- 35,000 sq m warehouse, 2,500 sq m office space, 15 truck parking spaces, 45 car parking spaces
- Few local amenities; however, local shopping center to be completed in five years' time

Unit 3

▷ p. 30

Exercise 14 · File 3

You and your colleague have both viewed the same office property. However, your notes differ. Find the six differences by taking turns asking questions. Use the illustration and the words in the box to find the differences.

columns · entrance · landscaping · parking facilities and public transportation · signage · stories · sun shading

Use questions like "What does the entrance look like?" or "Is there … ?"

Unit 4

▷ p. 38

Exercise 12 · File 4

You are a client executive at KTO Bank and have a meeting with a client who is applying for a loan. Ask questions and take notes to assess the credit standing of the client's company.

Development type: ....

Equity: ....

Assets: ....

Track record: ....

Time required to review the loan application: 2 weeks

Unit 5

▷ p. 47

Exercise 11 · File 5

You would like to purchase a mixed-use building with shops and offices. You are meeting with the seller. The due diligence phase is complete, but there are a few points you want to negotiate before signing the purchase agreement.

Lobby
The lobby is still under repair (though was scheduled to be finished last month). You want a €40,000 price reduction.

Tenant
Vittorio Gigli, a bar owner, has not signed a contract yet and is to occupy the property in three weeks. You require a signed contract.

Monument status
You have discovered that part of the building has historic monument protection. This was never mentioned before. You are concerned that this will affect your future refurbishment plans.

Unit 6

▷ p. 54

Exercise 8 · File 6

You work for Media Xpress, a tenant in an office building in Vancouver. Call Hercules Real Estate Management to inform them of the problems in your building and request action.

Check with property manager:
- *leaky pipes (undichte Rohre) and damp basement walls (feuchte Kellerwände)*
- *defective light in entrance hall*
- *air conditioning does not work*
- *rent reduction?*

Partner Files

Partner B

Unit 1

Exercise 11 · File 1

▷ p. 12

You own a retail business for cell phones and electronics, and you're looking for a new location for your shop. Your real estate agent has suggested three locations: Centennial Harbor, Station Road, and Silicon Park. Ask questions about these locations, then decide which location is the most suitable for your needs.

Ask questions about

- parking
- other businesses in the area
- public transportation
- special features

Unit 2

Exercise 9 · File 2

▷ p. 21

You are an investor and receive a call from a real estate agent. Discuss your investment criteria. The agent will give you details on two properties. Decide which of the two properties you're interested in and arrange an appointment to view it.

Country: Germany, Austria, Switzerland
Property type: mainly commercial
Investment volume: approx. € 35m
Location factors: close to shopping amenities, excellent transport links
Other preferences: modern, state-of-the-art, flexible

Unit 3

Exercise 14 · File 3

▷ p. 30

You and your colleague have both viewed the same office property. However, your notes differ. Find the six differences by taking turns asking questions. Use the illustration and the words in the box to find the differences.

columns · entrance · landscaping · parking facilities and public transportation · signage · stories · sun shading

Use questions like "What does the entrance look like?" or "Is there … ?"

▷ p. 38 Exercise 12 • File 4 **Unit 4**

You work for a development corporation. You have a meeting with a client executive at KTO Bank to discuss a loan application. The client executive will ask you questions about your company and your planned development. Here are some project details:

- Hotel and conference center
- Will be the company's second hotel development
- 520 beds
- Four large and eight small conference rooms
- €60m
- 10% equity
- Located near Schiphol Airport (the Netherlands)

Ask when you will find out if your loan application has been approved.

▷ p. 47 Exercise 11 • File 5 **Unit 5**

You are the seller of a mixed-use building with shops and offices. You are meeting the prospective buyer. A colleague has prepared the following memo for you.

Your negotiation partner may raise certain issues. I propose the following strategy:

- If they mention the repair work in the lobby, explain that completion will take another two months. If this is an issue, we can reduce the price by €30,000.
- Vittorio Gigli, the owner of the bar, has not signed a contract yet. He has been in Sardinia for six months, but he'll be back in two weeks. We can't reach him right now, but say that we'll try to speed up the signing process.
- If they mention the historic monument status, point out the advantages (it's a rare example of 1960s commercial architecture). If that doesn't help, reduce the price by €20,000.

▷ p. 54 Exercise 8 • File 6 **Unit 6**

You work for Hercules Real Estate Management and receive a call from one of your tenants. Ask for the information and explain to the tenant how the problems will be resolved.

Name ....

Location ....

Work to do ....

Phone number ....

Email address ....

Transcripts

Unit 1 Exercise 4

02

Well, I think that the importance of finding a good location can't be overestimated. It's like they always say: location, location, location. For example, the property needs to be highly visible. In other words, a large number of potential customers should be able to see your business.

Your location must also be easily accessible, either by public transportation or by car. The best streets, of course, are those with a lot of foot traffic. And if your customers are coming by car, you have to make sure there's a parking lot in the area.

You also need to find out what kind of people live in the neighborhood. What is their age? What is their income? That is, you need to learn about the demographics of the area.

The other thing you have to consider is competition. Are there other businesses nearby that will compete with you for customers?

So you see, there are many factors to consider when choosing a location. This is why doing a location analysis is so important before making a decision.

Unit 1 Exercise 10

03

Elizabeth Wow, what an amazing building! The space is so huge and bright, and the layout is perfect. How did you find it?

Olivia Well, I had tremendous help from the real estate broker. His name's Richard Hewes, and he helped me through the whole process.

Elizabeth Was it a lot of work, then?

Olivia It wasn't so difficult, especially since Richard provided me with a thorough location analysis.

Elizabeth A location analysis? What's that exactly?

Olivia Well, basically, it's a report that covers all the different factors you have to consider when choosing a property. For example, competition – meaning, if there are any other restaurants in the area.

Elizabeth But competition isn't always a bad thing, right?

Olivia Exactly. Other restaurants can help attract people to the area. In addition, you also have to consider demographics.

Elizabeth What do you mean by *demographics*?

Olivia You need to find out more about the people who live in the neighborhood: what kind of consumers they are, how old they are, and what their lifestyle and their purchasing power are like.

Elizabeth That sounds like a lot of research.

Olivia No kidding! And there's more, too. You also have to look at the foot traffic, which means the frequency of pedestrians in the area. And then there's public transportation and accessibility by car. What's the point of being located in a beautiful place if no one can get there? And what if they finally find your restaurant, but there are no parking spaces? You have to take everything into consideration.

Elizabeth Right, I see that. Did the agency do all the work for you, then?

Olivia Yes, they did all the essential research. But I also went and visited several locations myself, walked around different neighborhoods, and talked to other business owners.

Elizabeth Well, you've really done a great job. So, when do you think the restaurant will open?

Unit 2 Exercise 2

04

Julia Hello. Sorry I'm a few minutes late calling in. I was stuck in a meeting.

Kurt No problem. How's everything going?

Julia Oh, fine, thanks. It's just been a busy day!

Kurt Well, glad you could join us. Leah Taube is also on the line. She worked on an SPA for us last month, and is going to be handling our real estate investments from now on.

Julia Hi, Leah, nice to meet you.

Leah Likewise.

Kurt In fact, Leah and I were just discussing the new lease for the Lehmann property.

Julia Ah, of course. Let me pull that up on my computer as well. OK, here it is. I'm looking at the version that was emailed on Tuesday; is that the same one you have?

Kurt Yes, that's right. And basically everything looks good to me. I just had a few questions about some of the details.

Julia OK, what in particular?

Kurt Well, I think we should clarify certain aspects regarding tenant and landlord obligations for the property.

Leah Yes, I agree. For instance, there's a section on repairs. It should be much more detailed. It should specify who's responsible for repairs to broken or damaged fixtures.

Kurt I think there should also be more information about the service charges, and which costs are recoverable from the tenant.

Julia Those are all good points. Also, I was speaking to one of the prospective tenants this week, and he wanted to bring in an architect to make alterations to the space. I'm not sure that's covered in the lease.

Leah Actually, we have a section on alterations, if you look at the last paragraph on page three.

Julia Ah, yes, I see that now. But should that be expanded to include structural alterations?
Kurt Sorry, Julia, to include what?
Julia Structural alterations, such as changes to the roof, façade, or load-bearing walls.
Kurt Yes, that's a good idea.
Leah OK, well, I suggest I work on a new draft of the lease, if that's all right with you two. I can have it ready for you by next Friday.
Kurt That would be great – thanks, Leah!

Unit 2 Exercise 6

05

Julia Hello?
Leah Hello, Julia Lindsay, please.
Julia Speaking.
Leah Oh, hi, this is Leah Taube calling, the lawyer that Kurt Neumann has hired to help him with the Lehmann property.
Julia Yes, of course. I remember our conference call last week. How are you?
Leah Fine, thank you. Well, I just wanted to send you the latest version of the lease, but I don't seem to have your email address.
Julia Oh, no problem, I can give that to you. Do you have a pen?
Leah Yes, go ahead.
Julia It's j lindsay, all lowercase, at proglobal hyphen properties dot net.
Leah Great. Let me just read that back to you. That's j lindsay, j-l-i-n-d-s-a-y, at pro hyphen global hyphen properties dot net.
Julia Ah, no, proglobal is one word.
Leah Oh, I see: proglobal, one word, hyphen properties dot net.
Julia That's it.
Leah OK, terrific. I'll email that to you shortly.
Julia Splendid and thanks again.
Leah My pleasure. And if you don't receive the email, or have any trouble downloading the attachment, just let me know.
Julia OK, thanks. Bye now.
Leah Goodbye.

Unit 2 Exercise 7

06

1 leah underscore taube at fastmail dot c-h … that's leah, l-e-a-h, underscore taube, t-a-u-b-e, at fastmail, f-a-s-t-m-a-i-l, dot c-h
2 m dot pisecky at immob underscore advice dot a-t … that's m dot pisecky, p-i-s-e-c-k-y, at immob, i double-m o-b, underscore advice, a-d-v-i-c-e, dot a-t
3 andrew dot leicester at j-v-w dash consulting dot com … that's andrew, a-n-d-r-e-w, dot leicester, l-e-i-c-e-s-t-e-r, at j-v-w dash consulting, c-o-n-s-u-l-t-i-n-g dot com
4 ekkehardt dot richter at wohn underscore linie dot d-e … that's ekkehardt, e double-k e-h-a-r-d-t, dot richter, r-i-c-h-t-e-r, at wohn, w-o-h-n, underscore linie, l-i-n-i-e, dot d-e
5 j underscore sinha at ehouse dash corp dot i-n … that's j underscore sinha, s-i-n-h-a, at ehouse, e-h-o-u-s-e, dash corp, c-o-r-p, dot i-n
6 aaron dot portman at zinc dash holdings dot net … that's aaron with two a's, a-a-r-o-n, dot portman, p-o-r-t-m-a-n, at zinc, z-i-n-c, dash holdings, h-o-l-d-i-n-g-s, dot net
7 s dot oszevski at global estates dot r-u … that's s dot oszevski, o-s-z-e-v-s-k-i, at global estates, all one word, g-l-o-b-a-l-e-s-t-a-t-e-s, dot r-u
8 stephanie dash black at white dash gardens dot com dot a-u … that's stephanie, s-t-e-p-h-a-n-i-e, dash black, b-l-a-c-k, at white, w-h-i-t-e, dash gardens, g-a-r-d-e-n-s, dot com dot a-u

Unit 2 Exercise 10

07

Can you tell us which professionals are involved when people buy or sell property?

Well, there are a huge number of professionals in the real estate business and it would take too long to list them all. And very often, their responsibilities overlap.

Of course, it depends on what kind of property we're talking about. If a building is a new construction, you'll need architects to draw plans. Architects work very closely with contractors, who are in charge of the building site, the laying of the foundation, and the actual construction.

Another important person involved in a property is the surveyor. There are many different kinds of surveyors, but I'll focus on the valuation surveyor here. A valuation surveyor – known as an appraiser in the US – inspects the condition of the building, determines the market value of the property, and then produces a report of his or her findings.

Of course, we mustn't forget that there are many legal implications with real estate. That's why we need the assistance of lawyers. The degree to which lawyers are involved in the conveyancing process – that is, the process of property transaction – varies from country to country. A lawyer's responsibilities may include undertaking due diligence, doing title searches, and helping the client by drawing up contracts and so on.

Now, for the general public, one of the most visible real estate professions is probably that of the agent, sometimes known as a broker. He or she prepares the sales particulars, shows clients around properties, and helps them find the property which meets their requirements.

Let me also mention the acquisitions manager here. They identify potential investment opportunities and calculate how viable an investment might be.

Which professionals can offer assistance once you've already bought a property?

Well, again, there are many professions involved. If you've purchased real estate in order to generate rental income – say, an apartment building – you may be too busy to handle the administration yourself, so you'd ask a property manager to do the work for you. Property managers oversee payments, lease renewals, and the leasing of vacant property, and they are often in close contact with agents. They also liaise with contractors if needed – for instance, if a building has to be refurbished.

Unit 3 Exercise 5

08

A So, as you can see, the building is right on the main avenue here. But before we go in, let me just show you the entrance to the underground parking garage. It's just around the corner.
B Ah yes, I see it there. The garage is under the building, then?
A Yes, exactly. And there's also a full basement for tenant storage, as well as the furnace room. Now, let's go in the main entrance here. As you can see, there's a revolving door, and two standard doors as well.
B It's a nice lobby. Very high ceilings, aren't they?
A Indeed. That's one of the highlights of this building. And as you can see, there's the reception desk, and there's plenty of space for sofas and chairs as well.
B Yes, it's very nice. What else is on the ground floor?
A Down that hallway is the fitness center. We can take a look at that later. It's not very large, but of course it's a standard amenity in many large apartment buildings these days.
B I see there's a sprinkler system as well. Has that been installed throughout the building?
A Oh, yes, absolutely. For a building this size, it's required by law. Now, let's walk over to the elevators here, and look at one of the model apartments upstairs. There's also a service elevator, which is accessible through the back entrance.
B Great. Will we have time to look at the roof, too?
A Yes, if you like. We have a roof deck that's accessible to all tenants. The views are fantastic – you can see all the way across town to the river. Ah, there's the elevator now. After you …

Unit 3 Exercise 9

09

A Right, nearly there. Just to the right, OK? Here we are.
B Well, it's a big site. What about security?
A The site is fully secure. There's a perimeter fence as well as CCTV. As you can see, the building is located at the rear of the site, so there's plenty of space for the trucks to maneuver and enough parking for employees.
B Mm, does that mean that there are loading docks on only one side of the building?
A That's right. There are four roll-up doors in total.
B OK. And what's the clear height?
A Well, the doors have a clear height of six meters.
B Six meters – OK. You know that's important for a high-bay warehouse. What about the floor loading? When our pallets are stored on the racks, they can weigh up to five tons.
A That shouldn't be a problem. The floor load capacity is 30 kilonewtons per square meter, which is the industry standard. Let's go inside and have a closer look at the floor. The employee entrance is at the rear of the building, so if we go this way … OK, the gross internal area is 1,300 square meters, and as you can see, there are very few columns.
B That's certainly important if we're going to make efficient use of the space.

Unit 3 Exercise 12

10

1 This office building has approximately fifteen thousand square feet of leasable area.
2 The clear height is three point four five meters.
3 The usable area is twenty-three thousand, five hundred square meters.
4 The floor loading is twenty-five kilonewtons per square meter.
5 The size of the container is three by six by eight meters.
6 The property we are going to sell has a usable area of eighty-four thousand, five hundred and fifty square feet.
7 The clear height is exactly five point seven five meters.
8 The surveyor has measured the land, and it's exactly twelve thousand, five hundred and thirty square feet.
9 Standard wood pallets measure one hundred and fourteen by one hundred and twenty-two by twelve centimeters.
10 Revenue increased by three and a quarter percent last year.

Unit 4 Exercise 3

11

Andreas Hello, Mr. Woodrow, please take a seat. Would you like a cup of coffee?
Glen Actually, could I have a glass of water, please?
Andreas Yes, of course. Here you are.
Glen Thanks.
Andreas Right, so I've heard that you've completed two developments in Hungary?
Glen Yes, a shopping center and a shopping mall.
Andreas They're close to Budapest, aren't they?
Glen Exactly. In fact, the mall is fully leased now, and we've just signed a ten-year lease on the shopping center.
Andreas All right, so how can I help you today?

Glen Well, as I already mentioned on the phone, we're now looking for financing for a new shopping center near Prague.
Andreas OK. Could you tell me more about it?
Glen It's quite an exciting project. It's not in the city itself, but rather near the airport, where there's been a lot of growth recently.
Andreas And how large will the project be?
Glen The investment volume is €35 million, and we actually have enough equity available to finance the project independently. However, we're interested in exploring other possibilities as well to diversify our partnerships and to improve our leverage.
Andreas Yes, I see. What percentage of equity capital would you be able to provide?
Glen We were thinking 20%.
Andreas Hmm ... OK. Well, let me ask you another question, then. What additional collateral would you be able to offer?
Glen We have an undeveloped greenfield site in Hungary which is of considerable value. And we have a large logistics center near Budapest.
Andreas Fine. So let's focus on using those properties as collateral, then. Perhaps you could send me further details?
Glen Of course.
Andreas And in Prague, have you already pre-leased some of the space to tenants?
Glen Yes, as a matter of fact we've got a supermarket as our anchor tenant. We're also in negotiations with some electronics retail chains.
Andreas That's good to hear. Well, it sounds like a very promising project. Once we've received further details, we can discuss the term sheet.
Glen Wonderful. I'll make sure you get everything soon.

Unit 4 Exercise 5

12

1 one point four three percent
2 fifty-four divided by six equals nine
3 two hundred fifty thousand, six hundred and twenty-five
4 one million, five hundred forty-three, seven hundred and twelve
5 one thousand two hundred and fifty euros and forty-five cents
6 one million, four hundred thirty-five thousand minus two hundred thirty-three thousand equals one million two hundred and two thousand
7 annual return times a hundred divided by purchase price equals gross yield
8 zero point three percent of two point five million pounds

Unit 4 Exercise 6

13

The discounted cash flow method estimates the future income that an investment will produce, converting these future sums into present-day amounts.

The first step of this method is to calculate the present value of the income for each year.

In year one, the cash flow is estimated at €20,000. Multiplied by the present value of €1 for one year at 10%, this is 0.909. This produces a present value of €18,180.

In year two, the cash flow is estimated to be €40,000. Multiplied by the present value of €1 for two years at 10% equals 0.836. This produces a present value in year two of €33,040, and so on for each year ...

Finally, the total of all the discounted figures is calculated. These four years produce a present value of €99,290. The estimated sales price after four years is €88,000. The present capital value of the total investment is therefore €11,290.

Unit 4 Exercise 11

14

Our borrower is a subsidiary of NewShare Developments.

We've agreed to a 10-year maturity on the loan, but the borrower may request a five-year extension. The extension, however, must be arranged six months before maturity, which is the date at which the final repayment of a loan is to be paid.

It's important that the size of the loan is below the value of the completed development. It's quite common to get loans at a loan-to-value ratio of 60%, but for investments like this, the percentage is higher. The loan-to-value ratio for NewShare Developments is set at 75%.

We will require documents such as the articles of association and a company registration certificate before we proceed further.

In the event of default – meaning the borrower is unable to fulfill the loan conditions that were agreed to – the bank may repossess the property or other assets which were offered as collateral. This is known as foreclosure.

The arrangement fee is 0.15% of the total loan amount and is payable upfront, i.e., at the beginning of the loan period.

The term sheet will remain valid until the 21st of June.

Unit 5 **Exercise 5**

15

Due diligence is an important part of the transaction process and is undertaken before purchasing a property. Basically, it's important to investigate the asset to detect any risks that may be involved with the property. The due diligence period is often short, but to acquire and evaluate the materials requires a variety of specialists.

Part of the due diligence process involves checking the building's physical factors, and this is carried out by technical specialists. They inspect the construction type, the building itself, and the technical installations, such as the air conditioning and heating systems, to see if everything is in a good state of repair or if there are any defects. They will also determine if any hazardous materials, such as asbestos, have been used in the construction, and if there has been any contamination.

Other parts of the due diligence process relate to managing the legal documentation, and this is carried out by lawyers. A title search will be done – i.e., the lawyers will check that the seller is the owner. Lawyers will also verify that building regulations have been complied with, and check all tenant contracts to see if there are any limitations such as rights of way or restrictive covenants.

An acquisitions manager or real estate agent will often do the commercial due diligence. This involves analyzing the tenants' credit standing, the market situation, and other factors that affect the value of the property.

If any problems are identified during the due diligence phase, a reduced purchase price might be negotiated. If new information is found that strongly affects profitability, the buyer may even decide to stop the purchase.

Unit 5 **Exercise 8**

16

A All right, let's get started. As I mentioned, there are a number of issues we need to discuss before we can negotiate the purchase agreement. During the technical due diligence process, we identified a number of defects, and some of these could cost a considerable amount to repair.

B Really!

A Yes, one of our main concerns is the roof. We really must clarify this issue.

B Hmm … what would you suggest?

A Well, if we deducted the repair costs from the purchase price, we could come to an agreement on this point. Our engineers believe the costs will be about €100,000.

B You may have a point about the roof, but I think the repair costs your engineers have stated are too high. After we confirm the engineers' findings, I'd be willing to have the work carried out, provided that our contractors do the job.

A I think we can do that, on the condition that we have a clause in the agreement which details this issue.

B Well, I think I can agree to that.

A Good, that's agreed, then. The next thing we have to talk about is …

Unit 6 **Exercise 4**

17

How would you define property management?

There is no universal approach to managing property. And in fact, there is sometimes confusion about the definition of terms used to describe how properties are managed. For example, some activities within facility management may overlap with those in property management, and some activities in property management may overlap with asset management. In large organizations one employee might be responsible for just one area, such as maintenance or the budget, while in smaller organizations a few employees may be responsible for all aspects of the operation of property.

What is your approach at Curate?

Well, at Curate, our operations are divided into property management and facility management. Although, as I mentioned, there is often a lot of overlap between these two areas.

In general, the property manager is responsible for making sure the properties are run well as a business. This is mostly done at a regional level and involves liaising with tenants and owners, developing marketing strategies, keeping track of accounting, and cultivating new clients. Most of the time, the property manager works directly from our offices.

The facility manager, on the other hand, is regularly on site. He or she is looking after day-to-day maintenance, security, janitorial services, and so on. Our facility managers also oversee the various tradespeople such as plumbers and electricians that are contracted for specific jobs, and they make sure the work is carried out properly.

And to be effective in their jobs, the facility manager and the property manager have to be in touch frequently, and they often work together on specific issues.

What is the key to success in managing property?

Well, of course there are many important factors. But in my opinion, our number one responsibility is developing relationships. Communicating effectively and building trust with the client and the tenant is essential for every part of our work.

Unit 6 **Exercise 7**

Message 1 18

Hello, hello ... this is Paula Klinker from Menton and Johnson. We have a problem with the bathroom on our floor. The ceiling is damp. I think a water pipe has broken. Could you please send somebody up here as soon as possible? Oh yes, my phone number is 212 203 9290.

Message 2 19

Hello, this is already the second time I've called, and I hope it's the last. We could almost open a zoo with all the bugs around here. Someone's also seen a rat. You can't imagine how unbearable this has become for us here. There are children living here! I mean, would you want your child to grow up in this kind of environment? ... Oh yeah, this is Ben Randall, from New Riverside Apartments. You should have my number, but just in case, it's 661 483 2288.

Message 3 20

Hi. This is Nigel from accounting. Tip-Top Cleaning Services has sent us a letter. They claim you've agreed to their price increase, but I haven't seen anything in writing. Could you give me a call back ASAP? Thanks. Bye.

Message 4 21

Hello. This is Julia Bradman from Outdoor Stores. I'm calling regarding the reminders for rent payment which we keep receiving for our stores in Penrith and Warringah. It concerns the rent for the first quarter in January. Our bank assures us that the money has been transferred. Could you please, please look into it? Again, this is Julia Bradman from Outdoor Stores, and my phone number is ...

Message 5 22

Hello. It's me, Prisha. Sorry to bother you, but the boss gave us the OK for painting the corridor, so could you call our usual painter about that and ... Well ... uh, the plaster in our office also has some cracks in it, so could you please take care of that as well? I think you have the number of the plasterer. Thanks a lot, and have a great weekend. Bye!

Answer Key

Unit 1

Warmer
Answers will vary.

Exercise 1
Residential property: apartment/flat, condominium/commonhold, house, townhouse / terraced house
Commercial property: hotel, office space, logistics center, shopping mall / shopping centre

Exercise 2
Answers will vary.

Exercise 3
2 e (H) 3 f (B) 4 a (F) 5 d (G) 6 b/g (D)
7 h (C) 8 b/g (E)

Exercise 4
1 B 2 A 3 B 4 A 5 A

Exercise 5
(suggested answers)
1 visibility 2 accessibility, foot traffic, parking facilities, 3 demographics 4 competition

Exercise 6
1 by 2 at 3 to 4 on 5 of 6 opposite 7 near

Exercise 7
Answers will vary.

Exercise 8
1 process 2 protected 3 construction 4 structures
5 standard 6 reviewed 7 conditions 8 permits

1 F 2 F 3 T 4 F 5 T

Exercise 9
1 listed building (c)
2 alterations (b)
3 subject to conditions (d)
4 demolition (a)

Exercise 10
1 f 2 d 3 e 4 a 5 b 6 c
Not mentioned: quality of schools, distance to central business district, distance to parks, low crime rate

Exercise 11
Answers will vary.

Language of Business

German	AE	BE
Fachmarkt-zentrum	strip mall, shopping center	retail park
Einkaufszentrum	shopping mall	shopping centre
Kaufhaus	department store	department store

Unit 2

Warmer
1 appraiser 2 banker 3 owner 4 lawyer 5 agent

Exercise 1
1 credit standing 2 title deeds 3 comply with
4 refurbish 5 opportunities 6 vendors 8 negotiate

D acquisition manager
C loan officer (in a bank)
E asset manager
B developer
G real estate agent/broker
F property lawyer
H city/town planner

Exercise 2
1 stuck in a meeting
2 new lease
3 what in particular
4 broken or damaged
5 alterations to the space
6 load-bearing walls

Exercise 3
(suggested answers)
2 Oh, I'm afraid I'm totally tied up this week. Is Monday convenient for you?
3 Yes, that suits me fine. How about 11:30?
4 Certainly! What time would be convenient?
5 Yes, 8:00 is fine.
6 How about my office?
7 Yes, of course. It's Tellweg 120.
8 Sure, no problem. T-e-l-l-w-e-g.
9 Yes, I look forward to it.

Exercise 4
Answers will vary.

Exercise 5
1 ~~bureau~~ office
2 ~~date~~ appointment/meeting
3 ~~handy~~ cell phone / mobile
4 ~~actual~~ current

1 Your cell phone / mobile is ringing!
2 Please call my office.
3 Please tell me about the current status of the project.
4 I'd like to send you the sales details / rental details for this property.

Exercise 6
To: jlindsay@proglobal-properties.net
Subject: New version of the lease (suggested answer)
1 mentioned 2 specifically 3 clarify 4 repairs
5 particular 6 finalize 7 feedback 8 regards

Exercise 7
5 j_sinha@ehouse-corp.in
6 aaron.portman@zinc-holdings.net
7 s.oszevski@globalestates.ru
8 stephanie-black@white-gardens.com.au

Exercise 8
1 What type of property are you currently looking for?
2 What geographical regions are you focusing on?
3 What volume of investment did you have in mind?
4 What level of occupancy do you require?
5 What are the most important location factors?

A Country (2) B Location Factors (5)
C Property Type (1) D Investment Volume (3)
E Occupancy Rate (4)

Exercise 9
Answers will vary.

Exercise 10
agent/broker: 8, 9, 11
lawyer: 3, 5, 10
architect: 4
building contractor: 2, 15
appraiser: 14, 16
property manager: 1, 6, 13
acquisitions manager: 7, 12

Unit 3

Warmer
Answers will vary.

Exercise 1
1 townhouse / terraced house 2 business park
3 warehouse 4 apartment building 5 single-family house / detached house 6 office tower

Exercise 2
1 d 2 b 3 c 4 a 5 e

Exercise 3
1 completion 2 insurance 3 grades 4 location

Exercise 4
1 d 2 b 3 c 4 a

Exercise 5
1 lobby 2 elevator 3 revolving door 4 reception desk 5 parking garage 6 basement

Exercise 6
Answers will vary.

Exercise 7
1 factory 2 story 3 prestigious 4 corridor
5 hallway 6 representative 7 floor 8 fabric

Exercise 8
1 e 2 b 3 a 4 d 5 f 6 c

1 rear/back entrance 2 perimeter fence 3 CCTV
4 loading dock 5 roll-up doors / roller shutter doors
6 open-plan office 7 external sun shading
8 suspended ceiling 9 signage 10 cellular office
11 reception/lobby

Exercise 9
Mentioned: CCTV, clear height, columns, floor load capacity, parking, perimeter fence, racks, roll-up doors
Not mentioned: landscaping, net internal area, office space, refurbishment, signage

Exercise 10
1 There's a perimeter fence as well as CCTV.
2 The building is located at the rear of the site.
3 There are four roll-up doors in total.
4 The doors have a clear height of six meters.
5 There are very few columns.

Exercise 11
1 columns 2 raised floor 3 perimeter fence
4 open-plan office 5 landscaping
6 external sun shading 7 pallet racks/bays
8 cellular office

Exercise 12
1 fifteen thousand square feet
2 three point four five meters
3 twenty-three thousand, five hundred square meters
4 twenty-five kilonewtons per square meter
5 three by six by eight meters
6 84,550 sq ft
7 5.75 m
8 12,535 sq ft
9 114 x 122 x 12 cm
10 3.25%

Exercise 13
2 g G 3 d C 4 f E 5 c A 6 a D 7 e H 8 h B

Exercise 14
Answers will vary.

Unit 4

Warmer
(suggested answer)
4 – 2 – 5 – 3 – 1

Exercise 1
1 F 2 T 3 F 4 F 5 F

Exercise 2
The comparative method: price, basis
Discounted cash flow (DCF): income, value
The residual method: potential, site

Exercise 3
Type of Property: shopping center
Location: near Prague, near airport
Investment volume: € 35 million
Equity: 20 %
Tenants: supermarket, possibly electronics retail chains
Previous developments: shopping center and shopping mall in Hungary

Collateral: undeveloped greenfield site in Hungary and logistics center near Budapest

Exercise 4
1 T 2 E 3 N 4 A 5 N 6 T
Solution: TENANT

Exercise 5
1 one point four three percent
2 fifty-four divided by six equals nine
3 two hundred fifty thousand, six hundred (and) twenty-five
4 one million, five hundred forty-three thousand, seven hundred (and) twelve
5 one thousand two hundred (and) fifty euros and forty-five cents
6 one million, four hundred thirty-five thousand minus two hundred thirty-three thousand equals one million two hundred and two thousand
7 annual return times a hundred divided by purchase price equals gross yield
8 zero point three percent of two point five million pounds

Exercise 6

Cash Flow Statement			
Year	Cash Flow	Discount Factor 10% (present value of €1 at 10%)	Present Value
1	€20,000	0.909	€18,180
2	€40,000	0.836	€33,040
3	€44,000	0.751	€33,044
4	€22,000	0.683	€15,026
			€99,290
		Less outlay	€88,000
		New present value	**€11,290**

Exercise 7
1 g 2 b 3 a 4 c 5 f 6 e 7 h

Exercise 8
2 balance sheet, profit and loss statement 3 assets, collateral 4 liquidity 5 credit standing 6 cash flow

Exercise 9
(suggested answers)
1 We've arranged monthly installments.
2 Could you lend me your dictionary until tomorrow?
3 We need to borrow more capital (in order) to finance this project.
4 I started (out) in the real estate industry/sector.
5 Online banking has caused many bank branches to close.

Exercise 10
1 take out 2 secure 3 repay 4 refuse to grant
5 reschedule 6 default on 7 call in

Exercise 11
4 Articles of association 6 Arrangement fee
5 Collateral 3 Loan-to-value ratio 2 Maturity

1 a 2 f 3 e 4 b 5 d 6 c

Exercise 12
Answers will vary.

Unit 5

Warmer
1 letter of intent 2 due diligence 3 tenant agreement
4 negotiation

Exercise 1
a view b submit c undertake d receive
e negotiate f sign g hand over h enter into

Exercise 2
1 d 2 a 3 e 4 c 5 b

Exercise 3
1 inspection 2 approval 3 freehold 4 leasable
5 parking spaces 6 service charges 7 title
8 terms and conditions 9 deed of transfer 10 party

Exercise 4
1 bear the costs 2 rental income 3 draw up a contract 4 is subject to the terms and conditions
5 binding agreement

Exercise 5
1 F 2 T 3 T 4 T 5 F

Exercise 6
1 construction type – T
2 technical installations – T
3 state of repair – T
4 hazardous materials – T
5 title search – L
6 building regulations – L
7 rights of way – L
8 restrictive covenants – L
9 credit standing – B
10 market situation – B

Exercise 7
(suggested answers)
1 In the UK, the rent for commercial property is described on an annual basis; in central Europe, on a monthly basis.
2 Rent is usually adjusted every five years. This procedure is called "rent review".
3 Lease contracts differ in the level of costs (property tax, insurance, maintenance, and repair) that have to be paid in addition to the rent.
4 Triple net lease.
5 An American system for increasing rent, which is related to the consumer price index (CPI).

Exercise 8
Phrases used: 2, 4, 6
1 issues 2 suggest 3 agree 4 deducted
5 agreement 6 condition 7 clause

Exercise 9
1 owned, would build
2 accept, will sign

3 would consider, had
4 had, would pursue
5 would accept, were

Exercise 10

2 If you decontaminate the site, we can accept the purchase price.
3 If you get approval from a structural engineer, we will approve your application for a conversion.
4 If I had €5 million, I would buy a villa in Munich.
5 If you had an anchor tenant, we would invest.
6 If you provide more collateral, we'll finance the project.

Exercise 11

Answers will vary.

Exercise 12

1 in accordance with 2 legal right of ownership
3 burdens 4 from 5 guarantees 6 inform 7 paid

Exercise 13

1 T 2 F 3 T 4 T 5 F 6 F

Exercise 14

(suggested answers)
1 The client hasn't paid the commission for this property yet.
2 This office building isn't profitable for us.
3 We want to achieve a yield of 6%.
4 "The prospects / prospective clients seem reputable (to me)." – "Are you serious?"

Unit 6

Warmer

Answers will vary.

Exercise 1

1 compliance 2 pest control 3 procurement
4 landscaping

Exercise 2

1 founded 2 based 3 headquarters 4 divided
5 employs 6 portfolio

Exercise 3

Answers will vary.

Exercise 4

1 F 2 F 3 T 4 T 5 F

Exercise 5

2 d 3 c 4 a 5 f 6 b

1 develop a budget
2 measure the performance
3 provide information
4 negotiate contracts
5 oversee tenant moves
6 hire contractors

Exercise 6

1 F 2 G 3 C 4 E 5 B 6 D 7 H 8 A

Exercise 7

(Suggested answers)

Message 1

Name: Paula Klinker from Menton and Johnson
To Do: Water pipe broken, contact plumber and painter.
Phone Number: 212 203 9290

Message 2

Name: Ben Randall from New Riverside Apartments
To Do: Bugs and rats in the apartment, contact pest control.
Phone Number: 661 483 2288

Message 3

Name: Nigel from accounting
To Do: Tip-Top Cleaning Services. Accounting has nothing in writing about the price increase. Contact Nigel ASAP.
Phone Number: not mentioned

Message 4

Name: Julia Bradman from Outdoor Stores
To Do: Rent paid but still getting rent reminders for stores in Penrith and Warringah. Check with accounting, then call back.
Phone Number: not mentioned

Message 5

Name: Prisha
To Do: OK to repaint corridor and fix cracks in office. Contact painter and plasterer.
Phone Number: not mentioned

Exercise 8

Answers will vary.

Exercise 9

1 maintenance 2 cleaning 3 recovered 4 tenants
5 benefit 6 dispute 7 estimate 8 accounting

Exercise 10

(suggested answers)
1 Service charges are the costs for work such as repair and maintenance to the property and for the provision of heating, lighting, cleaning, security, etc.
2 The costs cannot be increased for profit.
3 Costs in multi-tenant buildings are shared.
4 Management provides an estimate of service charges to ensure transparency.

Exercise 11

2 Accounting fees 3 Electricity 8 Cleaning
13 Elevators and escalators 17 Public liability

Exercise 12

1 10 2 16 3 7 4 11 5 12 6 18 7 14 8 8
9 2 10 1 11 3 12 13

Exercise 13

1 ~~technique~~ technology
2 ~~caution~~ deposit
3 ~~controlled~~ checked
4 ~~economic~~ economical
5 ~~isolated~~ insulated

Phrases to Use

The phrases below will be useful tools in your work. Highlight phrases that are particularly relevant to you and look at them regularly to help you remember them.

Saying where things are

There is a building *by* the lake.
The gym is *on* the second floor.
The town is located *on* the A 25.
The office complex is *on* the River Thames.
Our office is *opposite* the supermarket.
The parking lot is *across* the street.
The balcony *faces* west.
If you're hungry, there's a nice restaurant *nearby*.
There's a bus stop on that street, and a subway station is also *nearby*.
The hotel is *near* the business park.
The business park is *near* the airport.
Winchester is / lies (to the) *west* of London.
The site is a few miles *east* of the village.
New York's Battery Park is on the *southernmost* tip of Manhattan.
This window *faces* north.

Asking questions about a location

What's the floor space?
How large is it?
How many square meters is it?
Is it close to public transportation?
How far is it from the city center?
What kind of parking facilities are there?
What other businesses/companies/stores are nearby?

Describing a location

The building is 1,000 square meters / has 1,000 square meters of usable space.
It's located directly on the harbor.
There are several subway/bus lines nearby.
It's near / close to / adjacent to / next to the train station.
There is a parking lot/garage across the street.

Polite language

Offering help

What can I do for you?
How can I help you?

Suggestions

How about …?
Would … suit you?
Is … convenient for you?

Requests

Could I possibly …?
Could I ask you to …?
Is there any chance …?
I was hoping …
I was wondering if …?
Would you mind …?

Softening bad news

Sorry, but …
I'm afraid … (I can't make it on Friday.)
Unfortunately, …
Actually, …

Confirming

Yes, of course.
Sure, no problem.
Certainly!
Two o'clock is fine.
I look forward to seeing you then.

Describing property

Describing general location

The building is right on …
It's just around the corner.
The office complex is situated in …
The retail warehouse is located in …

Describing the layout
This property comprises/features/offers ...
The building is equipped with many amenities.

Describing the location of rooms
Down that hallway is ...
The garage is adjacent to ...
This room leads directly to ...
Their offices are directly off the lobby.

The language of Negotiation

Expressing agreement
That sounds fine.
Yes, I think we can accept that.
I'd be willing to ... provided that ...
That seems perfectly reasonable to me.
I have no objections to that.
Yes, I am happy/satisfied with that.

Expressing partial agreement
I tend to agree with you, but ...
I see what you're saying, but ...
That might be true. However ...

Expressing disagreement
I'm afraid we can't accept that.
I'm afraid that is out of the question for us.
Unfortunately, we don't see eye to eye on that.

Clarifying
We really must clarify this issue.
So, if I understand you correctly ...
Could you expand on that?

Offering a compromise
We are prepared to offer ... if you ...
We are ready to ... on the understanding that ...
We are happy to offer/give you ... if ...
We can accept that, provided ...
I'm willing to ... , provided that ... / as along as ...

Presenting your company

The company was founded/established in ...
The company is based in ...
The company has several branches in ...
The headquarters ... is/are in ...
Our services include ...
We offer ...
We have a portfolio of ...
Our company is divided into ... departments.
We employ ... / The company employs ...
We have annual sales / an annual turnover of ...

Key Verbs in Context

to borrow sth.	The firm had to borrow € 100,000 to pay for refurbishments.	sich etw. borgen
to call in (a loan)	The bank sent us a letter calling in the loan, but our lawyer is going to discuss other options with them.	(Darlehen) kündigen
to carry out	In Germany, all property transactions are carried out by a certified notary.	ausführen
to compete	We can't compete with the other stores here and are relocating to another neighborhood next month.	in Wettbewerb stehen
to comply with	If you don't comply with local building regulations, you could face fines or even demolition.	(Gesetz, Bestimmung) befolgen
to decline	The number of available rentals has declined significantly since the beginning of the year.	zurückgehen
to default on (a loan)	The owner defaulted on the loan in January, and he's been in negotiations with the bank since then.	in Zahlungsverzug geraten
to draw up (contracts)	I think we found the ideal tenants, and our lawyers are drawing up contracts now.	(Verträge) aufsetzen
to keep track of sth.	One of my main responsibilities is to keep track of rental contracts.	etw. im Auge behalten
to lease (AE)	The law firm decided to lease 10,000 sq ft of space in the new office tower.	mieten
to lease (AE) / to let (BE)	Construction hasn't been completed yet, but we are already leasing space to future tenants.	vermieten
to liaise with/ between	As a property manager, I liaise between the client and the tenants.	in Kontakt sein
to monitor	In New York City, the Department of Buildings is in charge of monitoring all construction projects.	beobachten
to negotiate	We're negotiating a new purchase price after discovering the property had two restrictive covenants.	verhandeln
to refurbish	Our client plans to refurbish the property as soon as the current lease runs out.	sanieren, renovieren
to rent	We wanted to rent 20 parking places for our employees, but they only had five available.	mieten
to rent (out)	My landlord is renting out the first floor to a new grocery store.	vermieten
to repossess	After the owner missed multiple mortgage payments, the property was repossessed by the bank.	in Besitz nehmen
to reschedule (a loan)	Following a serious downturn in the market, we negotiated with the bank to reschedule our mortgage.	umschulden
to restore	We want to restore this historic building so it can be used as a restaurant and retail outlet.	wiederherstellen
to secure (a loan)	Once the loan was secured, we hired a firm to undertake due diligence on the property.	einen Kredit (be)sichern
to take advantage of sth.	They strongly recommend taking advantage of the current low interest rates.	Vorteil aus etw. ziehen
to take into account	Make sure to take into account future maintenance when calculating the cost of new buildings.	berücksichtigen
to take out (a loan)	I suggest talking to a bank officer now to see if you're eligible to take out a loan.	(einen Kredit) aufnehmen

American English vs. British English

American English	British English
apartment	flat, apartment
appraiser	valuer, valuation surveyor
bathroom	toilet, W.C.
apartment building	block of flats, apartment building
cell phone	mobile
condominium	commonhold
elevator	lift
foot traffic	footfall
ground/first floor	ground floor
highway, freeway, expressway	motorway
lawyer, attorney	lawyer, solicitor
to lease	to let
loan association	building society
main street	high street
parking lot	car park
real estate agent, realtor, agent	estate agent, agent
registry of deeds	Land Registry
roll-up doors	roller-shutter doors
seller	vendor, seller
shopping mall	shopping centre
sidewalk	pavement
single-family house	detached house
store	shop, store
strip mall, shopping center	retail park
subway	underground, tube
townhouse	terraced house
traffic circle	roundabout
zip code	post code

A–Z Wordlist

A

absorption Absorption, Absorptionsrate
accommodation Unterkunft
accomplishments Leistungen
acquisitions manager Akquisiteur
adjacent to neben
agent Immobilienmakler
alteration Umbau, Umgestaltung
amenities Annehmlichkeiten, Freizeitanlagen
anchor tenant Ankermieter
annual return Jahresrendite
ant Ameise
apartment Wohnung
to **apportion** (Kosten) umlegen
appraisal Bewertung
appraiser (AE) Immobiliengutachter/in
arrangement fee Bearbeitungsgebühr
articles of association Gesellschaftsvertrag
ASAP (as soon as possible) so bald wie möglich
asset manager Asset Manager, Anlagenverwalter
assets Vermögenswerte, Aktiva
assets and liabilities Aktiva und Passiva
assumed angenommen
attorney (AE) Rechtsanwalt

B

back Rückseite
balance sheet Bilanz
basement Untergeschoss
to **beat around the bush** um den heißen Brei herumreden
bike lane Radweg
binding (rechtlich) bindend
board (of directors) Vorstand
to **borrow sth.** sich etw. borgen
borrower Kreditnehmer
branch Filiale
broker Makler
building services technician Haustechniker/in
business park Gewerbegebiet
to **call in (a loan)** kündigen (Darlehen)

C

capital gain Veräußerungsgewinn
car park (BE) Parkplatz
caretaker (BE) Hausmeister
carpenter Zimmermann
to **carry out** ausführen
cash flow Cashflow/Geldfluss
caution Vorsicht
CCTV Videoüberwachung
cellular office Einzelbüro
central business district (CBD) zentrales Geschäftsgebiet
city limits Stadtgrenzen
city planner Stadtplaner/in
clause/terms of contract Vertragsklausel
clear height lichte Höhe
coat of paint Anstrich
collateral Sicherheit (bei Krediten)
column Säule, Pfeiler
commission Provision
commonhold (BE) Eigentumswohnung
comparative method Vergleichswertmethode
to **compete** in Wettbewerb stehen
competition Konkurrenz
compliance Einhaltung
to **comply with** befolgen (Gesetz, Bestimmung)
condominium (AE) Eigentumswohnung
to **conduct** durchführen
confidentiality agreement Geheimhaltungsabsprache
conservation area geschützter Bereich
consideration Abwägung, Prüfung
consumer price index (CPI) Verbraucherpreisindex
contamination Altlast(en)
contract Vertrag
contractor Bauunternehmer/in
conveyancing Eigentumsübertragung
corridor Flur
costs incurred angefallene Kosten
courageous mutig
covenant Vertragsklausel
crack Riss
credit standing Bonität
cul-de-sac Sackgasse

D

day-to-day (tag)täglich
to **decline** zurückgehen
deed of transfer Übertragungsurkunde
to **default on (a loan)** in Zahlungsverzug geraten
demolition Abriss
department store Kaufhaus
deposit Kaution
detached house Einfamilienhaus
developer Bauträger/in, Projektentwickler/in

discount factor Abzinsungsfaktor
discounted cash flow interne Zinsfußmethode
disposable income verfügbares Einkommen
disposal Veräußerung, Verkauf
distribution Vertrieb, Logistik
to **draw up (contracts)** (Verträge) aufsetzen
due diligence Due Diligence, sorgfältige Prüfung

E

earplugs Ohrstöpsel
easement Grunddienstbarkeit
electrical outlet Steckdose
electrician Elektriker/in
elevator Aufzug
enclosed inliegend, überdacht
encumbrance Grundstücksbelastung
to **enjoy the right to do sth.** das Recht haben, etw. zu tun
equity Eigenkapital
escalation Anstieg
escalator Rolltreppe
estate agent (BE) Immobilienmakler
exaggerated übertrieben
exhaust Abgas
existing building Bestandsimmobilie
extension Verlängerung der Laufzeit
exterminator Kammerjäger
external sun shading Außenjalousie
extraordinary außergewöhnlich

F

fabric Stoff, Material, Bausubstanz
façade Fassade
factory Fabrik
feasibility study Machbarkeitsstudie
fee Gebühr, Honorar
financial strength Bonität
fixtures Ausstattung
flat (BE) Wohnung
flood Überschwemmung
floor Etage, Stock
floor load capacity Bodenbelastbarkeit
foot traffic Passantenfrequenz, Fußgängerverkehr
foreclosure Zwangsvollstreckung
foundation Fundament
freehold Grundeigentum
frequency Häufigkeit
fulfillment Ausführung
furnace Beheizungsanlage

G

to **gazump** entgegen vorheriger Zusage das Objekt an einen Höherbietenden verkaufen
to **get rid of** loswerden, entsorgen
glare grelles Licht
gloomy düster
greenfield Neubauland, auf der grünen Wiese
gross brutto

H

hall(way) Flur
harbor Hafen
hard-nosed abgebrüht
headquarters Zentrale
heating Heizung
hereinafter im Folgenden
high-bay warehouse Hochregallager
human being Mensch

I

impressed beeindruckt
inaccuracy Ungenauigkeit
to **insulate** isolieren
insurance Versicherung
interest rate Zinssatz

J

janitorial services Hausmeisterdienste

K

to **keep track of sth.** etw. im Auge behalten

L

Land Registry (BE) Grundbuchamt
land use Flächennutzung
land-use plan Bebauungsplan
landscaper Landschaftsgärtner
landscaping Landschaftsgestaltung
lawyer Rechtsanwalt/Rechtsanwältin
layout Grundriss, Zimmeraufteilung
to **leak** undicht sein
leasable mietbar
to **lease (AE)** (ver)mieten, pachten
lease Mietvertrag
lease renewal Mietvertragsverlängerung/-erneuerung
leasehold Erbaurecht
lender Kreditgeber/in
less outlay abzüglich Auslagen
lessee Mieter/in
lessor Vermieter/in
to **let (BE)** vermieten
letter of intent (LOI) Absichtserklärung
leverage Hebelwirkung
liabilities Passiva
to **liaise** in Kontakt sein

lien Grundpfandrecht
likewise ebenfalls
limited liability company (LLC) GmbH
liquidity Zahlungsfähigkeit, Liquidität
listed building denkmalgeschütztes Gebäude
load-bearing lasttragend
loading dock Laderampe
loan Kredit
loan officer Finanzierungsspezialist/in
loan-to-value ratio (LTV) Beleihungsquote
lobby Eingangshalle, Foyer
location analysis Standortanalyse
logistics center Logistikzentrum
lowercase Kleinschrift

M

maintenance Instandhaltung, Wartung
maturity Fälligkeit
mixed use Mischnutzung
to **monitor** beobachten
mortgage Hypothek

N

to **negotiate** verhandeln
neighborhood nahe Umgebung
net netto
nitty-gritty wichtigste Punkte
no kidding! im Ernst!

O

occupancy rate Auslastung, Vermietungsstand
office tower Bürohochhaus
open-plan office Großraumbüro
outskirts Außenbereich
to **overestimate** überschätzen
overrated überbewertet

P

painter Maler/in
pallet Palette
parent company Muttergesellschaft
parking lot (AE) Parkplatz
pedestrian zone Fußgängerzone
perimeter fence Einfassungszaun
permit Genehmigung
pest control Schädlingsbekämpfung
pipe Rohr
planning board Bauamt
plant Fabrik
plasterer Gipser
pleasant angenehm
plumber Klempner/in
policy Versicherungspolice
to **polish** polieren
present value Barwert
press release Pressenotiz
prestigious repräsentativ
prime location 1A-Lage, Spitzenlage
prime rent Spitzenmiete
priority notice Auflassungsvormerkung
privacy Privatsphäre
procurement Beschaffung, Einkauf
profit and loss statement Gewinn- und Verlustrechnung
profitable rentabel
property manager Immobilienverwalter/in
prospective potenziell
provision Bereitstellung

R

rack Regal
raised floor Doppelboden
to **range between** sich bewegen zwischen
realtor (AE) Grundstücksmakler
rear Rückseite
reception Empfangsbereich
recoverable erstattungsfähig
to **refurbish** sanieren, renovieren
registry of deeds (AE) Grundbuchamt
regulations Bestimmungen
remaining restlich, verbleibend
to **rent** (ver)mieten
rent Miete
rental details Exposé
to **repossess** in Besitz nehmen
reputable seriös
requirement Bedingung
to **reschedule (a loan)** umschulden
residual method Restwertverfahren
residue Restwert
to **restore** wiederherstellen
restrictive covenant Nutzungsbeschränkung
retail chain Einzelhandelskette
retail park (BE) Fachmarktzentrum
retail warehouse Fachmarkt
return Rendite
revolving door Drehtür
right of first refusal Vorkaufsrecht
right of way Wegerecht
roll-up door (AE) Rolltor
roller shutter door (BE) Rolltor
roof Dach
roof deck Dachterrasse

S

sales details Exposé
to **scare the living daylights out of s.o.** jemanden zu Tode erschrecken
secondary location Nebenlage, B-Lage
to **secure** schützen
to **secure (a loan)** einen Kredit (be)sichern
service charges Nebenkosten
set forth wie dargelegt
sewage Abwasser
shelving Regale
shopping center (AE) Fachmarktzentrum
shopping centre (BE) Einkaufszentrum
shopping mall (AE) Einkaufszentrum
signage Beschilderung
single-story einstöckig
solicitor (BE) Rechtsanwalt
sought-after begehrt, gefragt
SPA (sales and purchase agreement) Kaufvertrag
sprinkler system Sprinkleranlage
stock bestehende (Miet-)Fläche
storage Lager
story (AE) / storey (BE) Stock
strip mall (AE) Fachmarktzentrum
structure Gebäude
stunning überwältigend
subsidiary Tochterunternehmen
subsoil Untergrund
subway (AE) U-Bahn
superintendent (AE) Hausmeister
suspended ceiling abgehängte Decke

T

to **take advantage of sth.** Vorteil aus etw. ziehen
to **take sth. into account** berücksichtigen
to **take out (a loan)** (einen Kredit) aufnehmen
take-up Flächenumsatz
tenant Mieter/in
tenant agreement Mietvertrag
term Dauer
term of loan Darlehenslaufzeit
term sheet Konditionenvereinbarung
terms and conditions Geschäftsbedingungen
terraced house (BE) Reihenhaus
tidy ordentlich
title deed Eigentumsurkunde
town planner Stadtplaner/in
townhouse (AE) Reihenhaus
track record Erfolgsbilanz
tradesperson Handwerker
tremendous enorm
turnover Umsatz
type of use Nutzungsart

U

to **underestimate** unterschätzen
underground (BE) U-Bahn
underscore Unterstrich
uppercase Großschrift
usable space Nutzfläche
utilities Versorgungseinrichtungen

V

vacancy Leerstand
vacant leer stehend
valuation Bewertung
value-added tax (VAT) Mehrwertsteuer
valuer / valuation surveyor (BE) Immobilien-gutachter/in
viability Rentabilität
visible sichtbar

W

warehouse Lagerhaus
waste removal Abfallbeseitigung
water damage Wasserschaden
weeds Unkraut

Y

yield Rendite

Z

zoning Flächenwidmung

Tracklist

Track	Unit	Exercise	Running time
01	Title/Copyright		0:54
02	Unit 1	Exercise 4	1:14
03	Unit 1	Exercise 10	2:06
04	Unit 2	Exercise 2	2:24
05	Unit 2	Exercise 6	1:33
06	Unit 2	Exercise 7	4:07
07	Unit 2	Exercise 10	2:40
08	Unit 3	Exercise 5	2:02
09	Unit 3	Exercise 9	1:38
10	Unit 3	Exercise 12	1:30
11	Unit 4	Exercise 3	2:13
12	Unit 4	Exercise 5	1:13
13	Unit 4	Exercise 6	1:28
14	Unit 4	Exercise 11	1:24
15	Unit 5	Exercise 5	2:00
16	Unit 5	Exercise 8	1:22
17	Unit 6	Exercise 4	2:37
18	Unit 6	Exercise 7 – Message 1	0:37
19	Unit 6	Exercise 7 – Message 2	0:48
20	Unit 6	Exercise 7 – Message 3	0:23
21	Unit 6	Exercise 7 – Message 4	0:35
22	Unit 6	Exercise 7 – Message 5	0:36
Total running time			35:19

Aufnahmestudio: New York Audio Productions